ep sport

netball

Rena B Stratford

Acknowledgements

The author would like to acknowledge with thanks the assistance of the following in the preparation of this book:

Alan Masters—sequence shots of skills

The players of the Bedfordshire County Association—pictured in the sequence shots

Gleaner Co. Ltd, Kingston, Jamaica—shots of international matches at the World Tournament of 1971

Jamaica Tourist Board—for the help of Roy O'Brien and Granville Allen

Bryn Campbell and the *Observer*—for the frontispiece

ISBN 0 7136 2573 2
Published by A & C Black (Publishers) Ltd,
35, Bedford Row, London WC1R 4JH.
Reprinted 1977
Reprinted 1981
Reprinted 1984

This book is copyright under the Berne Convention. All rights are reserved. Apart from any fair dealing for the purpose of private study, research, criticism or review, as permitted under the Copyright Act, 1956, no part of this publication may be reproduced, stored in a retrieval system, or transmitted in any form or by any means, electronic, electrical, chemical, mechanical, optical, photocopying, recording or otherwise, without the prior permission of the copyright owner. Enquiries should be addressed to the Publishers.

Copyright © Rena B. Stratford 1976, 1977, 1981, 1984

Text set in 11/12pt Monophoto Univers by G. Beard & Son Ltd., Brighton, Sussex. Printed and bound by Netherwood Dalton Ltd., Huddersfield.

EP Sport Series

All About Judo
Backpacking
Badminton
Basketball
Conditioning for Sport
Cricket
Field Athletics
Golf
Hockey for Men and Women
Improve your Riding
Men's Gymnastics
Modern Riding
Netball
Orienteering
Rugby Union
Snooker
Sports Acrobatics
Squash Rackets
Start Motor Cruising
Table Tennis
Target Rifle Shooting
Tennis up to Tournament Standard
Track Athletics
Trials Bike Riding
Underwater Swimming
Volleyball
Water Polo
Weight Lifting
Wildwater Canoeing
Women's Gymnastics

Foreword

The author of this book, Miss Rena Stratford, is internationally known as an expert physical educationalist who has taught, coached and lectured in many countries throughout the world. She has coached players of a wide age-range and varying ability and by her knowledge and enthusiasm has encouraged them to improve their skills and thus add to their enjoyment of the game.

This book analyses and teaches the basic techniques of netball for both players and coaches and will be found useful at all levels. The many photographs give added interest and impact to the text and offer the reader many ideas.

It is hoped that this publication will further promote the popularity of netball and encourage players and coaches alike to achieve greater skill.

I regard this book as a valuable addition to netball literature.

MARY FRENCH
National Technical Officer
A.E.N.A.

CONTENTS

Preface	8
Equipment	9
Principles of Teaching and Coaching	13
The Objects of the Game	14
Teaching Movement Skills	**15**
The teacher or coach	15
Method	15
Ball Passing	**17**
Catching	17
Throwing	24
Teaching	34
Footwork	37
Shooting for Goal	**42**
Techniques	42
Outwitting the opposition	45
Attacking Skills	**50**
Receiving a pass	50
Attacking techniques	51
Cues	54
Use of space	55
Positioning	58

Defending Skills	**61**
Close marking and interception	63
Defending a player with the ball	66
Intercepting a shot at goal	71
Defending the shooter	74
Defending players without the ball	75
Defending the goal	77
The throw up	79
Strategy—Team Attack	**81**
Principles of team attack play	81
Basic systems	84
Half-court systems	85
Full-court systems	91
Basic circle play	102
Strategy—Team Defence	**105**
Man-to-man defence	105
Zone defence	108
The Coaching Programme	**112**
Beginners	113
More experienced players	114
Team selection	114
Principles of attacking skill	115
Principles of defending skill	115
Coaching an Elite Squad	**116**
The coach	116
The players	116
Match play	118
The captain	120

Preface

Individual and team sports have a valuable contribution to make to all those girls and boys, men and women who discover the fun, challenge and adventure in playing them. These are there for all whether they are engaged in competitive play at high levels or one of a group playing on their own on a piece of vacant ground.

Each individual will gain improved health, fitness and movement skills, while the development of social attitudes, life values and understanding of oneself will also be fostered. Activity as the key to well-being need not be only for those of school or student age. Older women should continue to take part in games, modifying them according to their own needs and interests, for, to quote, 'the human body does not wear out nearly as quickly as it can rust out'.

Being a team game netball has a special value in socialising the individual who, as a member of a group engaged in a united effort, learns to substitute the selfish 'I' for the finer 'we' drives in order to make her contribution. One learns the values of give and take which carry over into life. During adolescence, when the desire to belong to a gang or a club is intensified, group activities gain special importance.

In their free time people only do voluntarily those things which bring them joy and satisfaction. They will choose to play netball only when they have an interest in doing so or when they possess enough skill to gain real satisfaction from it.

Unfortunately, many youngsters and adults have a dislike for active sports stemming from experiences at school, when they may have been the victims of poorly prepared teachers. Such teachers either spend precious class time teaching intricate and isolated game skills, while rarely giving the pupils opportunity to use them in the game situation; or else they go to the other extreme, always setting students to play in a game, instructing them principally in the Rules—with their emphasis on what one may not do—and failing to teach mastery of the basic individual and team skills. Either approach will have resulted in a lack of enjoyment.

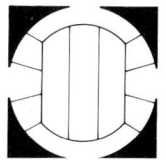

Equipment

One of the advantages of adopting netball as a sport for the individual is that no expensive personal equipment is required.

Dress

The player's outfit should be comfortable and allow freedom of movement. Traditionally it consists of:
- a *shirt*, preferably made of a material which will absorb perspiration
- a short *skirt*, usually pleated or wrap-around
- a *pullover*
- a *track suit*
- wool or orlon *socks*
- *shoes* which are light and supple. A good fit and good support for the ankles is most important. The soles must be slip-proof and hard wearing, since all play takes place on courts of hard surface. Shoes with leather uppers which have air holes are specially recommended to keep them dry and hygienic.

The well-dressed player

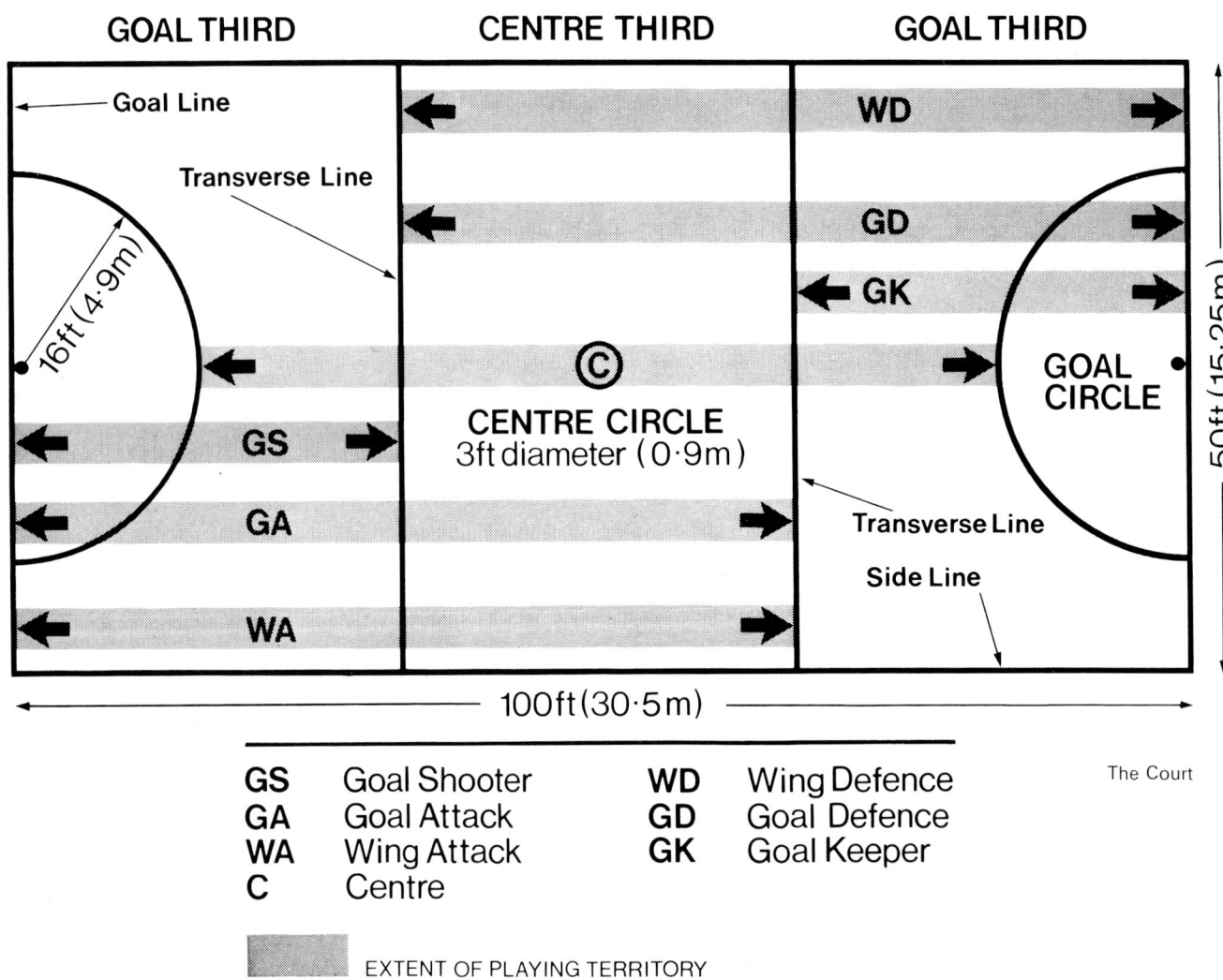

The Court

Netball can be played indoors on a wooden or composite surface, provided it is non slip. The surface of outdoor courts is hard and firm and non slip. There are many new proprietary materials which fulfil these conditions, some of which are porous to water. If non-porous they are laid to a fall to prevent puddles forming after rain. International rules lay down the measurements and markings of the court, which are shown on page 10.

Where space does not permit the laying of a full-size court, the game can be played on a smaller court, but it is recommended that the goal circles be of full size.

In some areas it is recommended that young children learn the game on a smaller court, but the advantages are debatable.

Ball

Although a ball is not an essential piece of personal equipment, there is great advantage, especially for a goal scorer, in possessing one of your own to practise ball-handling skills.

The Ball

The ball is a size five leather or moulded rubber ball, identical in size and weight with an Association Football. It should be kept well inflated, so that firm pressure with the thumb makes little indentation.

The Goal Posts

There are two goal posts placed one in the middle of each goal line.

The post may be supported by a socket in the ground or by a metal base which should not project on to the court.

Score Sheet

As used internationally (see page 12).

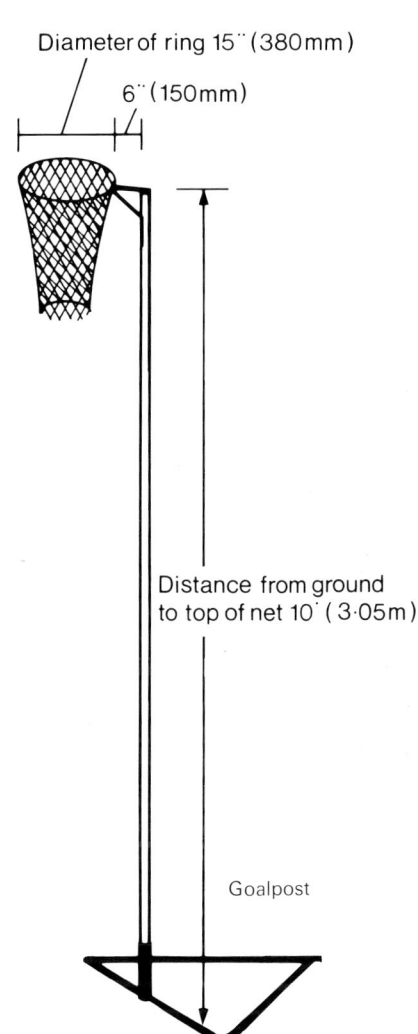

Umpires

There are two Umpires who officiate at a match. The game is under their control, and they must see that it is played according to the Rules.

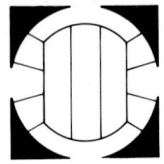

IFNA Scoresheet

Principles of Teaching and Coaching

Netball is a team game played almost entirely by women. It is governed by an International Federation which has a growing worldwide coverage of National Associations, giving opportunity for contacts between girls and women of different countries with the aim of promoting international understanding and friendship among the women of the world.

The opportunity to take part in international competition comes to few, but all players of all ages get enjoyment from participating in the game.

The technical details of the game will be explained more fully in later pages. By technique in sport is understood the ability to carry out specific movements to achieve the best results with great technical skill and the minimum expenditure of energy. For this, coaching is important—very important.

Since this book aims to assist the coach in her task to train players to be skilful as well as to help the player to help herself, we must consider some factors which contribute to the correct performance of any movement skill. A person's performance in a physical activity is limited by her physical strength and stamina, her reaction time, her motivation and (where tactics come in) her intelligence. All of these can be improved by suitable training, but they cannot be infinitely improved. However, although everyone cannot be turned into an International player, most people can be made much fitter, more active and more skilled, and that in itself is an admirable and worthwhile end. In the last two decades much research has been undertaken on the learning process, and the results of this suggests that in the teaching of netball, coaches would do well to consider the following basic factors:

1. Learning is mainly a doing, not a listening or watching activity.
2. In helping others to want to learn, motivation is of the utmost importance.
3. Lack of interest results in little learning.
4. Each student learns in her own way and at her own rate of speed.
5. Evaluation is an important part of all learning, for mistakes, when understood, play an important part in the mastery of any skill.
6. 'Practice makes perfect', but only if a student practises the correct pattern repeatedly in the right way, whereas practice of the incorrect can make faulty movement patterns permanent.
7. A skill learned in one situation will only be transferred to different situations if a conscious effort is made.

The Objects of the Game

A netball team consists of seven players, each of whom, by rule, has a limited area of the court in which she can operate, and a special role to play in the game.

The object of the game is that each team attempts to score goals by throwing the ball through the ring on top of the goal post. The team with the greatest number of goals scored is the winner. A team moves the ball towards the goal area by throwing and catching. No single player on her own can travel with the ball to the goal and score. There are rules associated with catching and throwing, one of which limits the amount of time a player may keep the ball in her possession to three seconds, which counts from the moment she gains control of the ball to the moment of release. There is also a limitation on the ground she can cover during that time. Two players only in a team have the role of shooting for goal. Obviously, only the team in possession of the ball is on the offensive and able to score. The aim of the opposing or defensive team is to attempt to gain possession of the ball and so become the offensive team in a position to move the ball and score.

Each player must learn certain specialised individual skills so that she can:
- throw and catch a netball with skill within the framework of the Rules
- make herself available against opposition to receive a pass from a team mate
- defend an opponent to intercept the pass to her.

The seven individual players dependent on each other to move the ball towards the goal must learn the team skills which enable a team to outwit and outmanoeuvre their opponents. Netball strategy involves great co-operation and understanding between all members of the team, one brilliant player being unable to make up for another's deficiencies. The teaching of strategy is an important task for the coach, and one made difficult by the many variables which present themselves in team play.

Teaching Movement Skills

Movement accuracy results from practising correct movement patterns until they become habitual. It is harder to unlearn or break a faulty movement and replace it with an accurate one than to learn the correct movement in the first place.

Although students can learn skills without a teacher, skill learning is more rapid and efficient if it results from copying, guidance, correction and instructor suggestion. Learning comes from trial, error and insight. Mastery comes through making mistakes.

The Teacher or Coach

The teacher must realise that all sports skills are based on movement factors which contribute to their correct performance. The following factors should be considered in the teaching of techniques:

1. **Strength** of muscle groups, especially of the **arms** to enable a player to throw the ball with speed and accuracy and to spin it to change its flight; strength of the **legs** to run with speed, to accelerate or decelerate, to reverse direction, and to lift body-weight for the elevation necessary to catch a high ball or intercept a pass.
2. **Energy** to provide stamina to maintain as full a work-load as possible over the whole of a match of four periods of fifteen minutes each.
3. **Flexibility** of the body to be able to bend and stretch and twist so that the whole body is used and contributes to the total sequence of events.
4. **Reaction time**, by which is meant the speed of responding to signals received through the eyes or ears.
5. **Vision**—to observe accurately, and focus attention on another player or on the ball; peripheral vision, which is the ability to see objects or movement over a wide field, so that a player can see the opportunities which present themselves in a game, and be able to make a choice from among all the variable options open to her.
6. **Concentration** on the tasks in hand throughout the period of play or practice; and the ability to obliterate disturbing emotional complications.
7. **Understanding** of the mechanics of a skill.

Method

The coach should bear in mind the factors affecting the learning of skills, as laid out on p. 13, and help the students accordingly.

Show and Tell

Verbal instructions before action should be kept to a minimum. Show and tell is the best way to get a message across effectively—but only if what is being shown is done correctly by the teacher for the student to copy, and the verbal explanation is quickly and easily understood. Teachers should master the art of saying much in a few words. Talk less and do more is a good motto to follow.

Practice

After the 'show and tell', students must try out what has been demonstrated. During this phase the coach must observe carefully the faults in each student's attempts, and patiently show each individual how she can improve.

Since praise is a great motivator, it should be given, or sprinkled, over all attempts to learn, but not to the degree that every attempt is 'good' for this could give the student a false standard of the skill expected. 'That was a good try' or 'That is an improvement' can brighten the attempts and quicken achievement when discouragement sets in after the student has been really trying.

Ball Passing

A skilful game hinges on effective passing to maintain possession of the ball. Passing the ball from player to player involves the basic skills of catching and throwing.

Catching

Catch the ball with two hands whenever possible, for two hands are safer than one. Dropping the ball or fumbling with it may cause your team to lose possession, or at least it may upset the timing of subsequent moves by your partners. The aim is to take possession surely, and throw accurately within three seconds of catching.

Eyes

Your eyes should follow the flight of the ball from as soon as it leaves the thrower's hands

Watching intently, the player follows the flight of the moving ball and judges its speed and direction

until you receive it safely. Judge the speed of the moving ball, and its direction and height.

Feet
Stand balanced on both feet. They should be comfortably apart one in front of the other, left foot in front.
Note: The description of footwork used for catching and throwing refers to right-handed players. Reverse left and right if left-handed.

Arms
Thrust the arms out towards the oncoming ball, so that the hands are just far enough apart to receive the ball; spread the fingers, while the palms of the hands face each other. The ball is caught by the fingers, thumb and heel of the thumb, not the palm of the hand; the thumbs behind the ball will prevent it

Catching

First the feet are correctly positioned, then the whole body is thrust upwards to reach the high ball

18   A brilliant catch ▶

from slipping through the hands. When catching a high pass the fingers point upwards; a chest-height pass, forwards, and a low pass, slightly downwards.
Slightly anticipating its touch, pull the ball in towards the body, applying the brake to halt it.
If arms and fingers are held stiffly they can receive painful damage from the impact of a forceful pass, while the ball rebounds away and the catch is dropped. As the arms 'give' so the body 'gives' also and the body-weight is transferred to the right foot.
It is not often that a player makes a catch in a stationary position as described, but it is best learnt this way first.

Eyes watching the ball, hands well placed with fingers spread

Tremendous elevation to meet the flying ball and make a sure two-handed catch. Notice fingers stretched and spread

Footwork

If the ball flies directly 'at' you, move into it by stepping forward with the left foot, taking the body-weight over it. Then transfer the weight back to the right foot as the arms and body 'give'.

A well-thrown ball to a moving player is one directed into the space ahead of her outstretched arms, at a height which will depend upon the opposition given. In this case, while watching the flight and direction of the ball, move to cut off its flight by making a long stride or forward leap. Thrust out the hand further from the ball to make the impact and follow quickly with the other hand to maintain the grip.

The footwork associated with the catch and following throw must be learnt and understood

Having made a long leap forward to catch the ball, this player lands on the right foot after thrusting the right leg well forward. She then grounds the left foot for balance, pivots on the right foot and steps with the left in the direction of the throw

in order that a player may comply with the Footwork Rule. Whether you are running to make a catch, or making a standing jump to catch the ball which rebounds from a shot, try to ground one foot first, and then ground the second foot in front to obtain and maintain balance and control. The rules allow you to use the second foot again several times in order to face another direction or turn round. Once the first foot is grounded, it can only be used as a pivoting foot to assist the stepping foot change direction. The pivoting foot may be lifted as a follow-through to the throw which follows the catch, but the throw must be made and the ball have left the hands before that foot is regrounded. For a right-handed thrower train yourself to land on the right foot first, bending

Two examples of a right-foot landing

the knee to prevent jarring your whole leg; ground the left foot to halt the momentum built up by your run and jump. Transfer the weight back to the right foot and step with the left or stepping foot in the direction you want to throw the ball. The right arm push and a step with the left foot helps you to be balanced and so aim an accurate throw. This follows what you instinctively do when you walk or run.

A skilful player has such control over her movements that she can land from her jump on either foot and so manage her weight and the placing of the other foot to throw so that the push of the throwing arm is balanced by the opposite foot.

All eyes watching the ball

Throwing

Once you have caught or held the ball it is said to be in your possession. The Rules of netball do not permit you to:
- drop the ball and recatch it
- bounce it and catch it again yourself
- throw the ball and touch it before another player has touched it.

A well-thrown ball is one which:
- the catcher is able to take
- is directed to the player best placed to receive it
- is thrown using the technique best suited to avoid interception by any opponent
- is so well timed that the catcher is free to take the ball against opposition and then make her throw within three seconds.

A skilful player has mastery of balance, control and rhythm.

The catch and throw then merges into one smooth and co-ordinated movement, carried out with speed and economy of effort. The learner should complete her catch with balance and control, pulling the ball into her body, and she should use the three seconds allowed her by the Rules to apply the correct techniques and make the necessary observations and preparations which will result in a 'well-thrown ball'.

The halt made between catch and throw is essential, so that you take time to make certain judgements. You must select not only the player who is free, but the player in the best place; you must judge the speed at which the selected player is moving, and take aim before delivering your pass. There are numerous ways of passing.

Having caught the ball and controlled her movement, WD is assessing the space into which to aim her throw

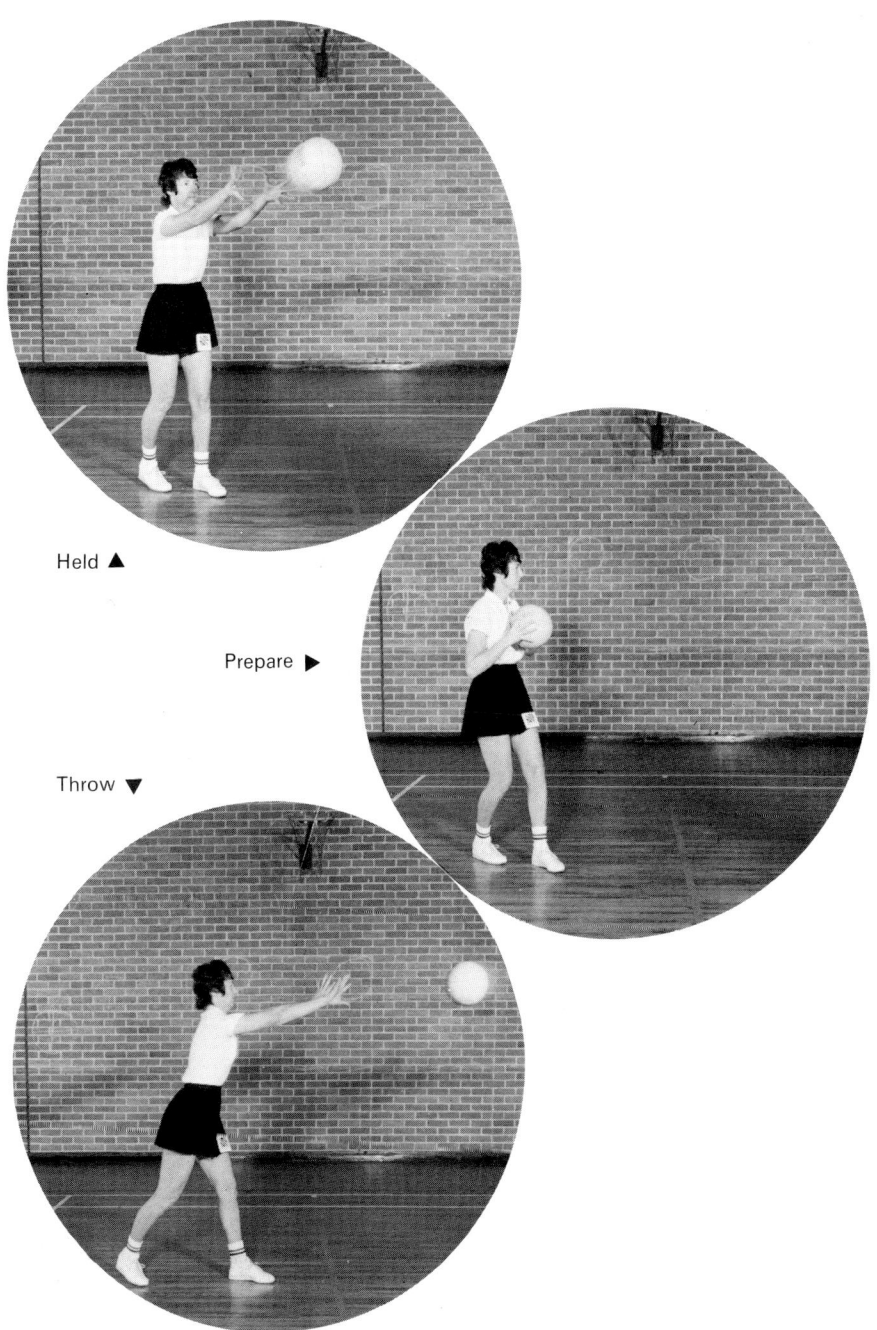

The chest pass

Held ▲

Prepare ▶

Throw ▼

The Chest Pass

A two-handed pass made at chest height. With the weight on the right foot and the ball held in two hands to the body, rotate the forearms to 'roll' the ball up to chest height, fingers pointing towards the head, thumbs nearly touching behind the ball; step with the left foot towards your target, transfer your weight to that foot and at the same time strongly stretch the elbows, and snap the wrists and thumbs to push the ball forward so that it travels directly to its target with speed and force. Keep the elbows down before and while the push is made. The chest throw is used when quick short passes are needed and there is no opponent between thrower and catcher. With quick reaction to the situation the ball is able to be released quickly because of the small movement of preparation to throw after the catch.

A chest pass into the circle. Notice the change of weight from right foot to left for force and snap

Shoulder pass

The Shoulder Pass

If the ball is to travel with speed to cover a longer distance, across the court or from centre third to goal circle, the best pass is by means of the shoulder throw, but again at the moment of throw the space between thrower and catcher must be clear, for with this pass the ball travels shoulder- to head-high and with power behind it.

Having caught the ball and completed the one–two landing, transfer the weight to the back foot. At the same time take the ball back with the throwing arm to turn you sideways on to the catcher. Release the front foot; thrust the throwing arm forward and bring the whole body into action to assist the push of the ball; make a strong thrust with the right leg right through the ankle and toes to throw the

Making a one-handed shoulder throw, the player is thrusting with the right leg and foot while placing the left in the direction she is aiming the pass

(a)

(b)

The shoulder pass

(a) Pass held, weight on left foot

(b) Pivot on right foot, ball held in one hand

(c) Ball pushed, weight transferred on to left foot in new direction

(d) Ball thrown with final snap of fingers

(c)

(d)

weight on to the left foot as it is placed well forward in the direction of the throw. The wrists and fingers give a final snap which spins the ball; the body turns forward as the right arm swings across the body as a follow-through.

The whole action is strong and powerful, well co-ordinated and yet rhythmical and smooth. The transfer of weight and the follow-through give you the impetus to move off at gathering speed to reposition yourself. If it feels safer and more controlled when taking the ball back preparatory to the throw, keep both hands in contact with the ball, then release the left hand just before the right hand pushes the ball forward.

◄
A good pass to the right to avoid interception by the waiting defender

The side pass

Side Pass

If when moving at speed the ball is caught at the side of the body use a modified chest pass or side pass. Lift the left elbow and bend the body to the right. The action of pushing the ball consists less of an elbow action as in the chest pass, and more of a strong turning and snapping of the wrists, which sends the ball at chest height directly to the catcher. The catch and throw merge into one continuous movement.

The thrower, C, is using a side pass to ▶ reach WA with the ball under the outstretched arms of a defender

The overhead pass

Held ▲

Prepare ▶

Throw ▼

The Overhead Pass or Lob

The overhead pass lobs the ball over the head and upstretched arms of an intercepting opponent to reach the catcher behind safely. This pass demands a clear judgement of the height and distance of the curved arc made by the ball during its flight. Having caught the ball, lift it high overhead, taking the weight back on to the back foot. Bend the elbows to lower the ball behind the head and transfer the weight on to the front foot. Push the ball upward by straightening the elbows and then swinging them forward from the shoulder. Release the ball as the elbows straighten. The arms are immediately above the head. A late delivery will bring the ball down.
Where your opponent is her required distance of three feet

A difficult overhead lob

(0.9 m) or more from the thrower's first grounded foot and the catcher is close behind her, the lob requires a delicate touch to clear the opponent and enable the catcher to take the ball with an upward jump. When the catcher moves away from the thrower she should run forwards with her head turned to watch the flight of the ball; you should in this case impart more forward thrust to the longer throw, when the arc made is flatter.

◀
An overhead throw to clear the waiting defender

The Underarm Pass

The underarm pass, in contrast to the lob, keeps the ball low, and is used to direct it under an opponent's outstretched arm. Make the pass by taking both arms back with elbows straight as the knees bend; the body crouches and the weight is taken on to the back foot; the ball is given a forward thrust as the weight is transferred forwards. Release the ball as the arms pass the side of the legs. A late release will lift the ball.

Should you catch the ball near the ground, a quick flick can direct the ball to a waiting catcher.

The underarm pass

Held ▶

Prepare ▲

Throw ▶

The Bounce Pass

The bounce pass will also keep the ball low—having drawn the ball to the waist on the catch, turn the ball as for a chest pass, but thrust the arms forwards and downwards, and the ball will pass under the outstretched arm of an opponent. The ball should strike the ground near to the catcher so that she can take it at hip height. With a turn of the wrists forward before the release top spin can be imparted to the ball, which makes it 'shoot' into the catcher's waiting hands; or a reverse turn of the wrists imparts back spin to slow down the forward rise of the ball, needed if the catch is moving fast towards the thrower.

The bounce pass

◀ Held

Propare ▲

◀ Throw

Teaching

Both the coach and the learner must realise that throwing and catching skills cannot be mastered within a short space of time, nor can they be learnt within the context of the game. The techniques must be isolated from the game, presented in their simplest form and developed through carefully planned stages.

Real mastery of the skill is only reached when it has been practised in its correct form so many times that it becomes a habit and can be applied without conscious effort in the game when under pressure from strong opposition with its attendant stress, tension and fatigue.

Those people who believe that they need only learn their positions on the court, places in the game and the Rules to be able to play are sadly mistaken. It is only natural that children want to play the game at once, and adults too for that matter. The difficulties of course are not realised until they try to handle the ball and manage their feet in making a contribution to their team's play.

An experienced coach will have discovered what for her is the best method of helping her students, but the generally accepted method of presenting both individual and team skills is by planning and using the following stages.

The first stage in learning ball passing between players is to teach throwing and catching as isolated skills. Being aware of the problems facing the thrower, the teacher must decide which of the six throwing techniques described she will teach first. My own personal view is that the two-handed throws, chest pass, lob, underhand pass and bounce are best taught first, because two hands are safer than one and because the thrower faces her target. The shoulder pass and

side pass should be used after the others have been mastered. The decision remains with the teacher, but whatever it is, she should be able to justify her decision. A student too, must know what is being done and why.
First present the skill by means of a clear demonstration, a film, a photograph or failing these, a brief description. Then organise the group for practice. Where sufficient balls are available practice in twos is ideal; whereas with the use of one ball only per fourteen or more players, learning is that much slower.
Practise in the simplest way, which is standing and throwing at a stationary target, which can be a wall or a stationary player. Both teacher and pupil must learn to observe and recognise faults, and correct them at once. Each skill is a chronological sequence of movement, and can be seen as preparation, action, recovery—look at each part. Because footwork and balance are so important in netball emphasise them and observe, correct and develop that part of throwing. Give praise and encouragement for improvement, and praise for good form, but realise that the correct form must be repeated many, many times before one can say it is learnt. Catch and throw must be taught together; they accompany and are dependent on each other.

Throwing Drills

1. A throws to B; B to C, etc.

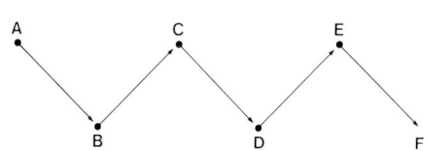

2. A throws to B, B to C, C to A. Different throws can be made from each position.

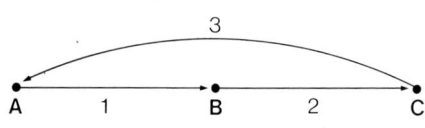

3. A passes to B and runs to stand in B's place; B passes to C, and runs to stand in C's place. Continue along the line and back.

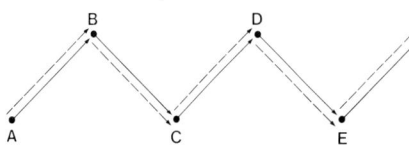

To maintain interest the practices can be made competitive by seeing who can complete the highest number of throws in 30 seconds, or who can be the first to complete so many circuits. When competition in this way is introduced, the conscious effort is one of speed, and correct form tends to be lost. Remember that it is important to use the feet correctly. When waiting to catch, face the thrower, stretch out your arms towards her, place your left foot in front of your right foot, with the weight over the left foot. As the ball is caught, take the weight back on the right foot, pivot on it, and as the throw is made step towards your target and take your weight on to the stepping foot.

4. Pass continuously against a wall, catching the rebounding ball, using the different types of pass. Then throw the ball to hit the wall at an angle so that you have to move to either side to make the catch. Reach for the ball to your right by stepping towards it with your left foot, putting your weight on this forward foot, and stretching your right hand out behind the flight of the ball to stop it. As the ball comes into the hand the whole arm and body must 'give' in the direction of the flight. The other hand is placed on the front of the ball to hold it.

Footwork

Seldom in a game of netball does a player receive a ball while stationary. She must use her feet with agility and control, and keep within the Rule governing the footwork of throwing and catching. When running to make a catch, it is the landing which plays an important part when a ball is caught. All players should be taught to land on one foot followed by the other, since this gives more freedom of movement. The landing foot is the pivoting foot and, when pivoting, keeps contact with the ground. The other foot is the stepping foot which may be used as many times as needed and in any direction to assist in gaining balance and control, and to give force and direction to the throw.

Footwork Practice

Run and leap and land right foot (left for left-handed players) followed by the left, allowing the weight to be over the left foot. As you leap into the air extend your landing foot out in front, to help you to slow the forward momentum of your run, and to be balanced, for the landing foot must be 'glued' to the ground to enable you to pivot with it, and it may not be 'dragged'. If you have a natural left take-off foot, a leap from it will naturally lead to a right-foot landing. If your natural take-off foot is the right, it is not difficult to learn to land on it—the movement is a hop jump. Since the hop occurs before the ball is caught, the movement does not break the Rule that hopping while the ball is in your possession is not allowed.

The foregoing footwork is used when moving to catch the ball. Practise first in this way:

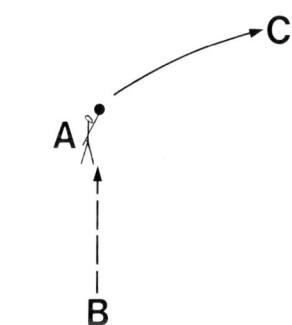

A stands with a ball held in one hand reaching with it as high as possible. B sprints towards the ball and leaps up and forward to snatch it from A's hand. She lands right foot, puts down left, pivots on the right and throws to C, stepping in her direction.

Catching a stationary ball enables the catcher to concentrate on her footwork.

An excellent pass ahead of the catcher

Thrusting the right leg forward brings the catcher into balance. She now assesses the movement of GS in order to place and time her throw

In a well co-ordinated throw the opposite arm and leg are thrust for balance with the right arm and left leg giving direction to the pass

The Use of Space

Having learnt **how** to throw and catch, you now learn to aim your throw in the right direction—the **where** of passing.

With the ball in the 'ready' position to throw, watch the catcher sprinting away from her opponent and try to assess her speed. Aim your throw into the space ahead of the catcher, so that with a long leap, and by stretching her arms forward, she can reach forward and stop the ball's flight with the hand farther from the thrower; she can then quickly move the second hand on to the side of the ball and make her catch. If she is running fast your aim must be ten feet (3.05 m) or so in front of the point she has reached when you release the ball. If your aim is poor, and the ball arrives to her body, there is a grave risk that the defending opponent will intercept the pass.

Practices

1. Work in pairs. A has the ball. Catcher B runs along line YX to catch the ball thrown ahead at X; she then pivots to face A, throws the ball to her and runs back to Y, receiving the ball back again. Use chest throw for short quick passes; shoulder throw if distance between A and B is greater.
This develops accurate throwing ahead, short, rapid runs and pivot turns.

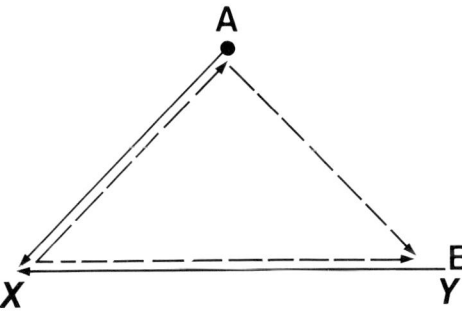

2. B runs across in front of thrower A who passes the ball ahead of her, so that she catches it at X, pivots and returns ball to A and continues on across the court to Y. A throws to C, D, etc. Return, running in the opposite direction in order to pivot to the right.
Catching on the move, passing ahead, and pivoting need constant practice. Remember to try and land on the right foot after catching, and to be balanced before pivoting to throw.

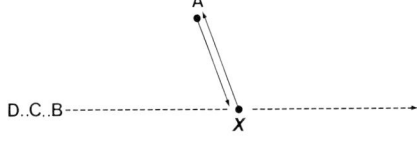

3. Use the last practice as for a pass from Centre to Wing Attack or Goal Attack.

4. Thrower A has the ball; the catchers are at Y side by side facing the line. Each in turn runs to catch at X, balances, pivots and passes back to A. Later, catchers line up at X and run to catch at Y and so run to the left.

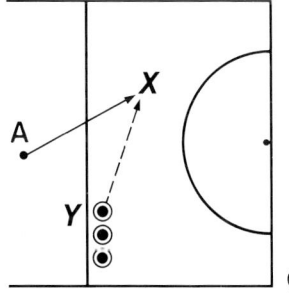

(a)

5. Similar situations as occur in the game can be used to practise angled passes ahead of a player as in Figs. (b) and (c).

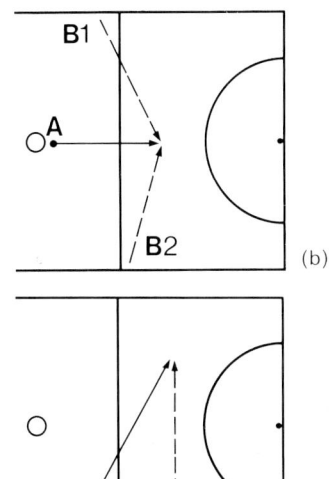

(b)

(c)

For example, Wing Attack throws from the goal third to Goal Shooter who runs from the goal third into the circle to receive her catch. When organising practice situations, work in small groups of two or three; if you place the thrower in the middle of the court, then place the catcher near the side line so that she runs diagonally towards the thrower, as in Figs. (a) and (b) rather than in (c) where the catcher runs *away* from the thrower, and both throw and catch are difficult to accomplish successfully.

Throwing and Catching Lob Passes

1. A_2 runs to catch pass made by A to B; B runs to C and catches the lob as ball thrown to C, etc.
To catch a lobbed ball, catcher moves away from the thrower but turns her head to watch the ball flight and time her jump.

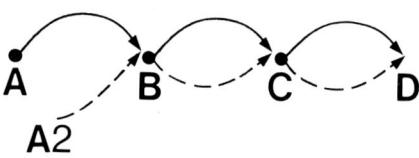

2. A with the ball lobs it over B to C as they turn to run away from A.

Bias Passing

Three players A B C (A with ball).
A throws to B at Z and then runs to X;
B throws to C at W and then runs to Y;
C throws to A at Z and then runs to X.

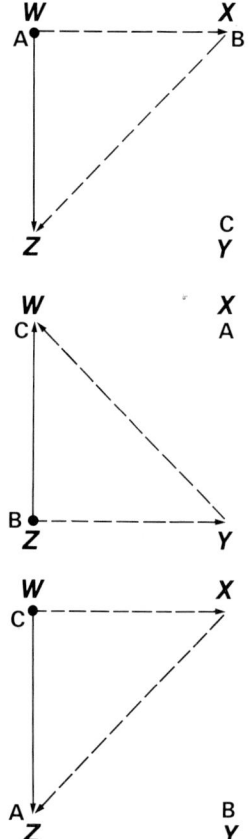

'Holding' the Run

Player A stands at X and B at Y. Player A passes the ball to Z where player B runs to receive it. Having thrown, player A must wait, or hold her run to Y until player B has made her catch, pivoted and is balanced ready to throw to A at Y, etc. Players tend to make their move to receive the ball too early, so remember to watch your thrower, while manoeuvring to throw off your opponent, and make your sprint run sudden and in the right direction, only when the thrower is ready to throw and looking in your direction.

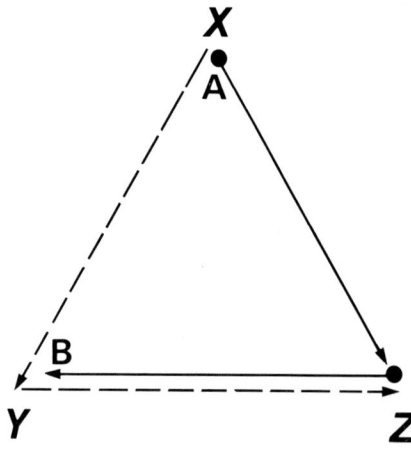

The attacking player (black) holds her run until the ball is caught by the thrower

A turning jump to catch the ball. With this turn the arms, hands and shoulders can control the direction of the ball and keep it moving to the next player

As you become skilful you can develop a smooth continuous movement which flows from the run into the catch and following pass. When you make your jump or the last long stride of the run to catch the ball, land on the right foot and pull the ball to the side of you. Use a side pass as the left foot is grounded. Or if the catch is made above the head, take the ball back and use an overhead pass. For your pass to be successful you must be aware of the positions and movements of your team players and opponents.

From the elementary level there must be a basic understanding of weight of body which should go into the landing, weight being taken forward on to the balls of the feet. With correct training, players should have little difficulty balancing in any situation on the court, or stopping suddenly, changing direction, intercepting, etc. Players must be brought to realise that it is important to catch, balance and throw, before they go on to achieve the much more difficult stage of a running style. The emphasis must first be on control rather than speed.

Shooting for Goal

Techniques

Goal shooting is a specialised throwing skill, in which only two players in a team, Goal Shooter and Goal Attack, can participate. An attempt at the goal may be made only from within the goal circle, situated at each team's attacking end of the court.

Before making a shot the Goal Shooter or Goal Attack must first receive a pass and make her catch with the same footwork as that described for catching, with the addition that both feet must be grounded within the boundary line of the goal circle (remember that the width of the line is included in the circle area).

At the beginners' level, an attempt should be made to teach all players the shooting techniques, in order to discover those players with the best shooting potential.

Skilful shooting requires a mastery of different techniques based on two fundamental qualities—balance and judgement of distance. The ring through which the ball must pass is ten feet (3.05 m) high, placed horizontally; it is projected forward six inches (150 mm) from the post and is fifteen inches (380 mm) in diameter, which is only a little larger than the ball. Therefore there is little margin for error. Accuracy must be complete when shooting for goal, whereas an inaccurate pass directed at a moving player, can, by the skill of the catcher, be made successful.

Successful shots at goal are the result of knowing where to aim and using the correct direction and degree of strength.

It is obvious that the shorter the throw the easier it is to be accurate. Any marginal error is magnified as the distance of the throw becomes greater.

First learn to shoot by standing in front, and not more than four feet (1.2 m) from the base of the post.

Different techniques of shooting are used according to the different situations a shooter faces in a game, her position in the circle, the type of pass made to her, the height and position of her opponent, together with her defending skill.

The throw for goal may be two-handed or one-handed. Although an individual matter for the goal shooter to decide, it is easier and sounder to learn with two hands first. Later, when some degree of accuracy is attained, the learner should try with one, and so find out the best style to suit her.

Basic Two-handed Shot

Stand balanced with your weight evenly distributed between your feet, and your left foot in front of your right. Hold the ball securely in two hands, with fingers spread and curved. Your thumb should be under the ball, your fingers behind the ball and your wrists cocked. Stretch your arms up so that the ball is held high above your head, out of reach of an opponent trying to cover the ball. Aim for a point above and in front of the ring so that it drops in a curve and falls through the ring.
The farther away from the post you are, the farther in front of the ring you must aim as the highest point in the curved trajectory of the ball's flight.
To push the ball upwards check that your body-weight remains

Two-handed shot, stepping back with left foot

A jump shot in which the arm is stretched and the ball released from as high a position as possible to prevent any interception

over your feet until the ball is released. From your upstretched aiming position, bend your elbows and lower the ball to just above head height, at the same time bending the knees. Then stretch your knees and push upwards with your arms and use an up and over action, following through with your arms, wrists and fingers. Some shooters keep the feet grounded during the whole shooting action, while others jump as they launch the ball towards the ring, to add power to the push.
Follow up your shot, whether successful or not, to secure the rebound.

A strong thrust from the ground has given good elevation while the right arm directs and adjusts ball flight and the fingers produce ball spin. The shooter's weight is still over her feet

Outwitting the Opposition

To outwit a defending opponent who is attempting either to intercept the shot or make it difficult for you to aim, you may have to change your technique. So long as you can catch the ball in the inner half of the goal circle you can follow the basic technique described, because the ball travels almost vertically upwards. Concentrate on holding the ball high, and unless she is much taller than you, your opponent will be unable to intercept the shot. From the outer half of the goal circle, and against a tall opponent standing poised in front of you, it is unwise to adopt the basic technique. The measures you can take to avoid possible interception are:

1. Vary the flight of the ball; aim for a higher point so that the ball rises more steeply from your hands.
2. Vary the timing of your action; aim carefully, then make a quick bend and push, stretching yourself up as much as possible.
3. Make a fake shot to upset her timing, and follow it with the real thing.
4. Make a backward step shot. Having moved in the circle to make your catch, land right foot then left foot, balance, lift the ball above the head; step back with the left foot, taking your body-weight back, bending the knee slightly, as you prepare to make the push with the arms. Keep the right foot grounded for balance. If you take too large a step back you will find you have a problem with the front foot; if you slide it back, you infringe the footwork rule. If, to avoid this you lift the front foot, you are unbalanced, standing on one leg, and the success of your shot is doubtful. The backward step increases the distance between you and your opponent, for she cannot follow you back.
5. Take your opponent unawares by stepping to the right, crossing the left foot over, pivot at the same time turning to face the ring, and shoot.
6. If you manage to leave your opponent behind by outrunning her, jump to catch the ball, turning to face the ring as you do so. Land on one foot, step and jump to shoot so that the whole run, jump, land and shoot becomes one continuous action without pause. Take the ball above your head from the catch to enable you to sight the ring and take aim. Keep balanced,

▲ Controlling the ball with both hands in order to move it safely out of reach of a defender

◀ A near shot for goal by GS being defended by the opposing GK, with GA and the opposing GD alert and positioned for the rebounding ball. There is no chance of interception, for GS is at full stretch and the ball travelling vertically

An aim and throw with one hand. The ball is raised as high as possible and is not lowered below head height during the preparation ▼

and check your weight from moving in front of your second foot too soon, otherwise you will overshoot the ring. Remember that you are allowed only three seconds from the moment you take possession of the ball until it leaves your hands in making the shot. Catch the ball and get it into the aiming position to give you a second to make your aim and gain control and balance.

The defender, GK, having placed her front foot three feet from the right foot of her opponent, watches the ball and prepares to make her leap to intercept the shot. Interception is avoided by a two-handed overhead shot with a step back to give more space

Running shot at goal ▼

GA has elected to shoot from the award of a penalty pass. Her step forward and jump has left her opponent behind and unable to move until the ball has left the shooter's hands, thus giving herself the advantage to catch the ball on the rebound should she fail to score.

Practices

1. Use chalk to mark numbers in the circle, placing them to cover the circle starting close to the post and finishing at the circle edge. Start at 1; after two consecutive scoring shots move to 2, etc.

3. The first thrower of the line stands outside the circle at C and throws the ball to the first of a line at A, who must catch it inside the circle, and shoot for goal. Both thrower and shooter follow in to catch the rebound, whether the score is made or not. The next pair repeat, etc.

4. B throws the ball to A who runs into the circle to catch. C takes up her position three feet (0.9 m) from A's landing foot and either remains there, or attempts to intercept. A shoots and both A and C run to catch the rebound. B joins the line of shooters, C becomes the thrower and A the defender.

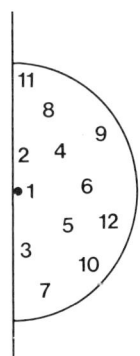

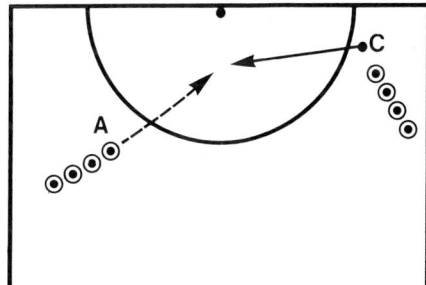

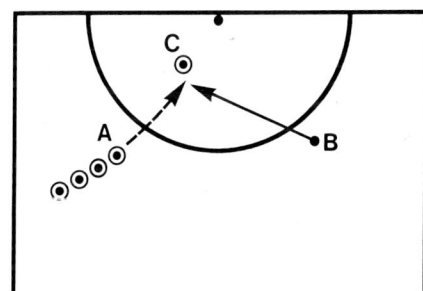

2. From a near position, shoot, move to retrieve the ball and continue. See how many goals you can score in one minute.

Attacking Skills

In order to play a part in team attack a player must be agile and skilful to free herself from an opponent and to move to receive a pass in the right place and at the right time.
Basic Skills must first be learnt, understood and practised so that the technique of attacking can be applied. These basic skills may be used with advantage as a warm-up at the beginning of a practice session, or before the start of a match:
1. Running fast, using short strides for short distances, and lengthening the stride for longer distances, with good use of knees and arms.
2. Running and stopping suddenly, by making a long last stride, thrusting the leg forward and grounding the foot strongly to check the forward momentum built up by the run.
3. Sudden changes of movement, speed and direction.
4. Acceleration and deceleration.
5. Running and leaping for length or height.
6. Bouncing, twisting, turning, bending and stretching of the body to make it flexible.

Give the players the experience of responding to signals to quicken their reflex actions and sense of timing. The coach must try and create an attacking attitude in her players, so that it is the ball that becomes all-important and not the defending opponent.

Receiving a Pass

To make yourself available to receive a pass, you must free yourself from your opponent, using a variety of techniques, each of which has its place according to the space you have available at the moment, the position of your opponent in relation to you, the court, the ball or the goal, and the skill of your opponent. Assume a starting position with feet slightly apart, knees bent and weight evenly distributed between the feet, on the balls of the feet. You may be motionless in the starting position, thus giving nothing away to the guarding opponent of what you are going to do, or when you will make your sudden move. You hold the initiative, the opponent is always the follower. She must therefore discover your intentions before she can make a move to follow your action. Some players find that they can spring into action more quickly if they flex their knees and bounce gently before making a sudden strong movement.

Sprint to one side

Attacking Techniques

1. Suddenly sprint to the free side, if your opponent is standing beside you and there is sufficient space on your free side, or forwards, when you will start level.
These starting positions are met with when players are lined up before a Centre pass.

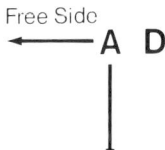

2. Turn about behind your opponent, and sprint away to your marked side. By moving behind her, your opponent is unsighted for a moment, which will delay her following action.

These 'feint' movements use the body to attract the defender to commit herself to move in one direction. The legs push from the ground to change direction

'Dodging'

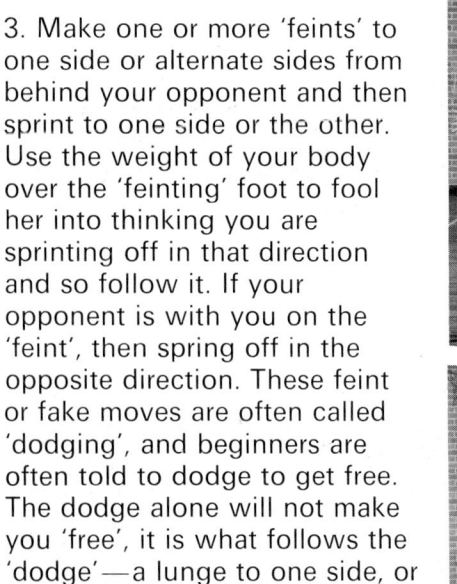

3. Make one or more 'feints' to one side or alternate sides from behind your opponent and then sprint to one side or the other. Use the weight of your body over the 'feinting' foot to fool her into thinking you are sprinting off in that direction and so follow it. If your opponent is with you on the 'feint', then spring off in the opposite direction. These feint or fake moves are often called 'dodging', and beginners are often told to dodge to get free. The dodge alone will not make you 'free', it is what follows the 'dodge'—a lunge to one side, or a sprint—which makes you free to receive a pass. The dodge upsets the defender's timing and sense of direction. By 'dodging' behind your opponent, she is unsighted.

Sprint off in one direction, stop and reverse

4. Sprint off in one direction, and if your opponent remains with you, suddenly stop and reverse direction, or suddenly stop, dodge back and run on.

5. If running 'neck and neck' with your opponent, suddenly stop and lunge with one foot in the direction from which you started your sprint. For this technique to be successful, you must sprint for a long enough distance to build up a momentum, otherwise your opponent will be able to hold back with you.

Once you are free, keep moving without lessening speed until you receive the ball. By slowing down or stopping you will lose your advantage, and become closely marked again, or your opponent will intercept the pass.

Getting free in the goal circle, GS grounds her right foot and lunges forward with her left to catch the ball. She then regains her balance and weight on the right foot. She thus obtains a position close to the post and forces her opponent to retreat to a distance of three feet from her right foot

Running towards her unmarked side to receive a safe pass, the player (arrowed) gives the cue of her intentions to the thrower ▶

Having caught the ball in the air the thrower must judge GS's direction of move before she lands herself. If she judges correctly her pass will not be intercepted by the opponent. GS must communicate in some way with C ▼

Cues

When making your move to draw the pass you must give a 'cue' to your thrower to help her to make her necessary judgements before throwing. In other words, you must make clear to her your intentions. As you start your sudden sprint, indicate your direction by thrusting out an arm. As soon as she appreciates your all-out effort to outrun your opponent she will assess your speed and direction, and make her pass. If your opponent remains level with you, you and the thrower must realise that the pass cannot be made with any degree of safety, so you must adopt technique (4) or (5) above and give your thrower an indication. The more skilful players become, the more quickly they can react to any situation that arises. From the start, the coach must help her players to give and 'read' the cues which every player must get from her team members. This is known as a sense of perception, or a 'games sense'.

Practices

1. Work in pairs, attacker and defender, standing side by side, spaced over the court; on a signal given by the coach, attacker turns and sprints to cross the side line before her opponent.

Practise running to left and to right. The signal to start can at first be a whistle or a call, to get the sudden reaction. Then change the audible signal to a visual arm signal, given by the coach. This trains the attackers to concentrate and use their eyes to watch the thrower. The sudden thrusting out of one arm towards the side of the court both gives a cue to sprint and the direction to move. Each of the techniques can be learnt in the same way, without the ball.

2. Work in threes, one thrower with a ball, one attacker and one defender.
Attacker A with Defender D between A and the ball. Use a dodge and sprint technique; T throws when A is free and indicates; A receives the ball, passes back to T and repeats. After a set number of attempts, each of the three players change roles, etc. Then confine the players to a small area in which to manoeuvre.
Set up suitable situations in which to practise the other techniques.

3. Two versus two, passing in a confined space using one technique at a time.

Use of Space

It is not only essential that each player learns **how** to get free from her opponent, she must also learn **where** to move in relation to the thrower. The attacker must try to direct her run so that when she is free to receive the pass, her defender is not positioned or moving between attacker and thrower.

1. A, the attacker, is moving away from the thrower, T, thus increasing the distance with each step. It is both a difficult throw and an awkward catch. In each direction the marker remains between ball and catcher and thus interception is very possible. (Fig. a.)

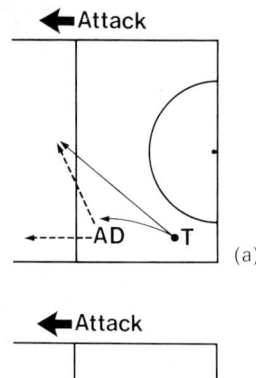
(a)

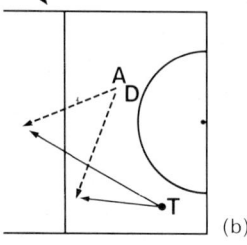
(b)

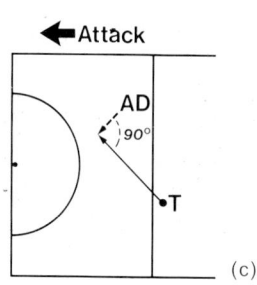
(c)

Where to attack. The attacker runs diagonally across her thrower ▼

Where to attack against opposition ▼

2. A, the attacker, runs across the thrower and makes her catch as she passes her, or soon after. If the thrower is delayed, the attacker increases her distance from T with each step. (Fig. b.)

From any position on the court an attacker has two alternative directions she can move so that she crosses the thrower.

For the easiest throw and catch, an angle of approximately ninety degrees between runner and ball flight is best. (Fig. c.)

Moving the ball through the centre third, WD-C-WA. Notice players moving across the court into space

Practices

Use can be made of the practices given on pages 39-40. The directions of the run to catch in those examples are repeated here to show the link between the two techniques. To link throwing, attacking and catching techniques, practise ball passing in twos or threes without opposition, concentrating on where to receive in relation to the thrower:

1. Free team passing two versus two.
2. Passing up court in twos without and with opponents.
3. Passing in twos as applied to certain situations in the game, e.g. GA to GS, C to WA, to move the ball in different directions in relation to the thrower and the court. In this way the practices will relate to the game.

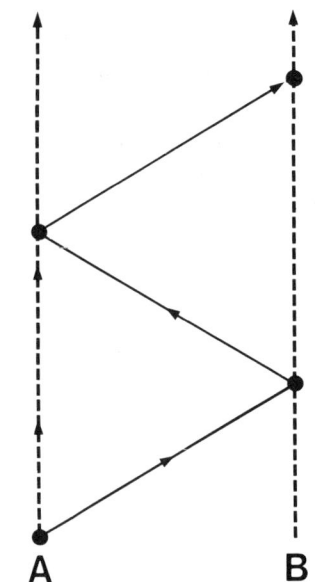

Positioning

Positioning is an important part of the skill of attacking. The technique is to move out of the space on the court in which you want to receive your pass and to create a space into which to run. A player playing in the Goal Shooter position is often guilty of standing in the circle near the post while the team attack is proceeding up the court, so that when her time comes to receive a pass, she has no alternative but to move away from the goal towards the circumference of the circle to make her catch. She thus gives herself a long shot, and allows her defender to come between herself and the goal.

'Positioning' yourself involves continuous movement and adjustment of your position on the court; awareness of other players in your group, and of crowded and empty spaces on the court. You need room to manoeuvre and space in which to run to receive your pass. This demands an awareness not only of empty space, but of the right space for each attacker as her turn arrives to receive a pass.

GA using the space in the circle to advantage. The pass beats the opposing GD and puts GA into a good shooting position

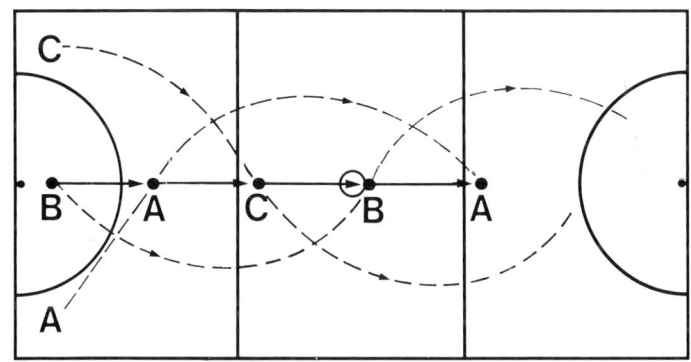

Practice

Three players, A, B, C, line up across a base line, B holding the ball. A runs diagonally across B to receive a pass ahead from her, as shown in the diagram. Meanwhile, C runs down her sideline so that when A has caught the ball she breaks into a sprint to make her catch straight ahead. In turn, B will have run from her starting position to receive from C, and so the process continues until the players run out of space. After positioning yourself, it is vital that you 'time' your move to make your catch. Hold your run as shown in 'Passing' until your thrower has safely caught the ball and is ready to throw, then make your sprint. If your opponent has maintained her close marking position when you are positioning yourself you will have to manoeuvre to free yourself. This you must do in time to start your sprint at the right moment.

The most common faults found when moving to receive the ball are:

1. Over-anticipating the throw, and sprinting too soon.
2. Creeping towards the place where you should be receiving the ball.
3. A failure to concentrate and to watch the ball.
4. A failure to assess the right time in the team attack to join it.

These faults will be eradicated when you understand team play and court-craft.

It is necessary when both attacking and defending to understand the Rule of Personal Contact. No player shall come into personal contact with an opponent in such a manner as to interfere with her play either accidentally or deliberately.

As an attacker tries to get free she may not push into or past her opponent, or trip her up or knock into her.

When running to catch a high ball she must not collide with an opponent. The runner carries the responsibility for contact with a stationary opponent, but if both are moving, or both jumping for the ball, the responsibility may be shared.

Defending Skills

In my opinion all the attacking skills of throwing, catching, footwork and getting free should be practised before any real defending work is started. Beginners have enough problems in achieving successful passes to one another, without having the distraction of a defender. Whatever stage of development a player has reached, she must taste success to be motivated into making further effort. Since anticipation and a sense of timing are most important in good defensive work, players in a game situation need to have instilled into them ideas of position, positioning and timing of moves, together with a positive approach to team attack. In so many elementary or average games, the players forget that the purpose of passing is to keep the ball in the team's possession, move it to the goal and score, and instead the game consists of players competing within each team to receive passes.

In a game of netball all players in a team, no matter in what position they play, must both attack and defend. When a team is in possession of the ball, every member of that team must attack, although not all at the same time; when possession of the ball is lost, every member of that team defends.

The aim of defensive play is to regain possession of the ball, in order to attack and score.

The method of defending used most successfully is a man-to-man or one-on-one defence, where each player makes herself responsible for defending her opponent.

An élite team can play a zone defence in which a defender works with other members of her team to guard an area of the court, and cut off any passes into her area.

The defending skill consists of:
1. Close marking. A defender stations herself close enough to an attacker to make other players uncertain whether the attacker can safely receive the ball. If the pass is attempted she should be able to intercept it.
2. When her opponent has successfully received the ball, the defender attempts to intercept the throw or shot after the ball has been released from the thrower's hands.

Good defending partnership. GK makes an excellent clean interception while her partner GD is on the alert to give support and at the same time has positioned herself to attack or defend the GS

Backing up

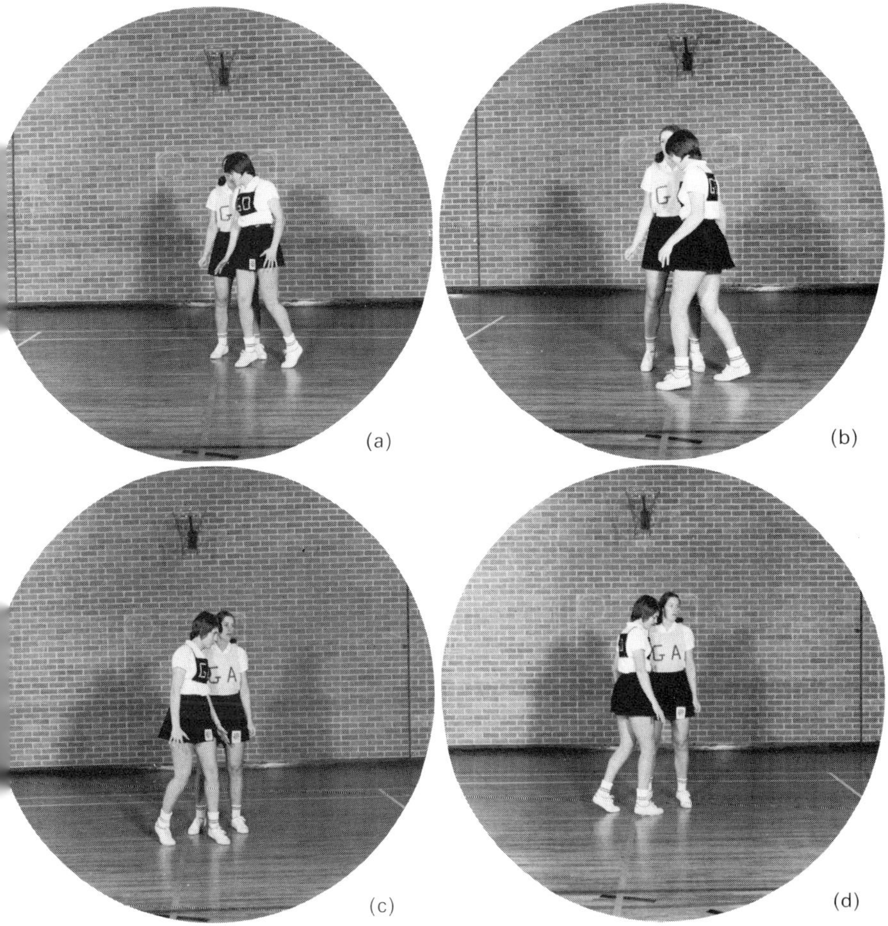

(a) (b) (c) (d)

(a) Position for marking, half-turned with right foot forward, which turns defender with her back towards the attacker. The left foot forward (b) turns defender towards the attacker. If the attacker is near the side line of the court (c and d), mark on the court side

Close Marking and Interception

Mark closely, placing yourself between your opponent and the ball; stand close, yet not so close that you risk contacting her, or causing contact.
Stand half-turned to face across her, your left shoulder covering her right; or face in the opposite direction with your right shoulder covering her left. Stand with your feet easily apart, the foot nearer your opponent in front and the other behind, which turns you slightly away from her. In this way you can keep both your opponent and the ball within your field of vision.
Keep your weight on the balls of the feet and your knees slightly bent so that you are ready to move or jump in any direction.

Good close marking by GD (arrowed) who has placed herself between her opponent and the ball, and is able to see both

Keep the arms down to avoid infringing the Obstruction Rule, which states that the arms may not be outstretched away from the sides of the body while the defender is closer than three feet (0.9 m) from her attacker.

As your opponent moves to left or right change direction with her by using very small, quick steps. Keep the front foot in front, instead of passing your legs as in running, so that you keep your weight between your feet and can change direction forwards and backwards maintaining your balance.

By keeping on the move you can keep her well covered as she manoeuvres and positions herself ready to make her lunge or sprint to receive the pass. Once you have anticipated the direction and timing of her run try and follow her closely.

Marking, with interception of the pass

Watch the ball closely from the moment it leaves the thrower's hands, assessing its direction and speed. Cease to pay attention to your opponent and go all out now to reach for the ball and so make your interception. You may thrust your arms out to do so. This action does not infringe the Obstruction Rule.
If you fail to make the interception, recover quickly and return to mark closely again.

◄
Close defending and attempt to intercept a pass to the nearer player

GK watching distance from landing foot

Practices

1. Work in pairs—an attacker and a defender (without a ball). Learn the marking positions, on both the right and left sides of the attacker. The attacker assumes the initiative; the defender must understand that her role is one of 'follower'. The defender practises the close following of a short sprint—a sprint, stop and continue; sprint, stop and reverse direction; dodge and sprint.
2. Work in threes—a thrower with the ball makes a pass to an attacker who frees herself using a stated technique; defender close marks and attempts to intercept the pass. Limit the attacker to a small area.
3. Any of the practices for attacking can be used for the practice of defending.

Defending a Player with the Ball

If you have failed to prevent your opponent from receiving the ball, then you must quickly recover from your attempt, and move rapidly to take up a position in front of the thrower, making yourself aware of your opponent's landing. In order to be free to make an attempt to intercept her throw you must place your feet at least three feet (0.9 m) away from her first landing foot after she catches the ball. If, however, she receives the ball with both feet grounded or jumps to catch and lands on both feet at the same time then the distance is measured between the foot nearer to you and your nearer foot.

GD has taken up the correct distance from her opponent's feet and is following the movement of the ball. She must be careful not to put her hands on it

Keep your body moving with arms and legs covering as much space as possible, and watch her movement of the ball while she prepares to throw. Try to assess the type of pass she will make and the direction, and then leap into the path of the ball as soon as it has left her hands. If she pivots before throwing, move round with her as she turns, so that you keep in front of her.

If your attempt to intercept the pass fails, then quickly close-mark your opponent again as she moves off to reposition herself after throwing.

A feint pass is difficult to cover, but try to follow the movement of her hands with yours. Remember that she must throw within three seconds of catching, so endeavour to cover her movements so effectively that you force a held ball, or a wild throw.

The defender forces her opponent to make an error by making a barrier with her arms while watching the player prepare to throw. Correct interpretation of the throwing action results in an interception

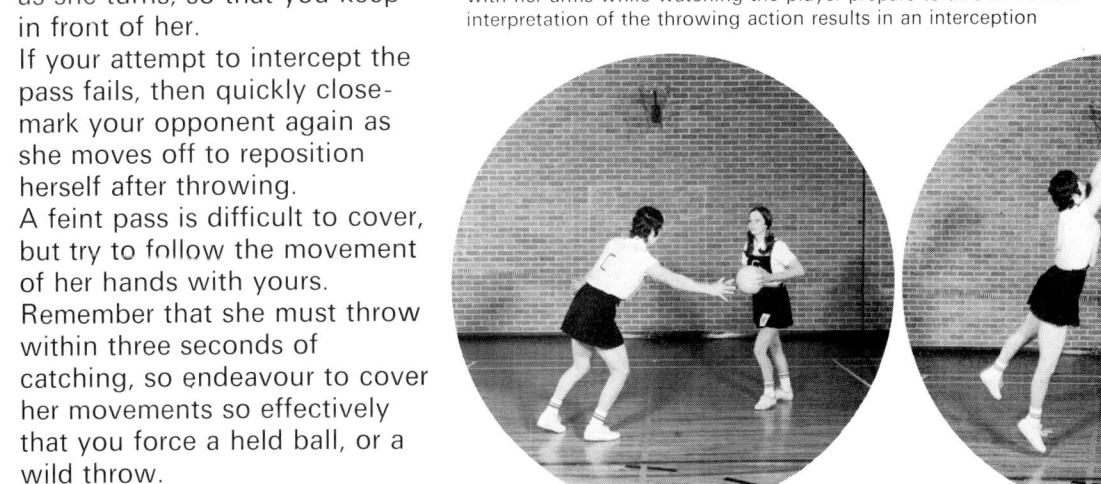

Interception of a lobbed pass ▶

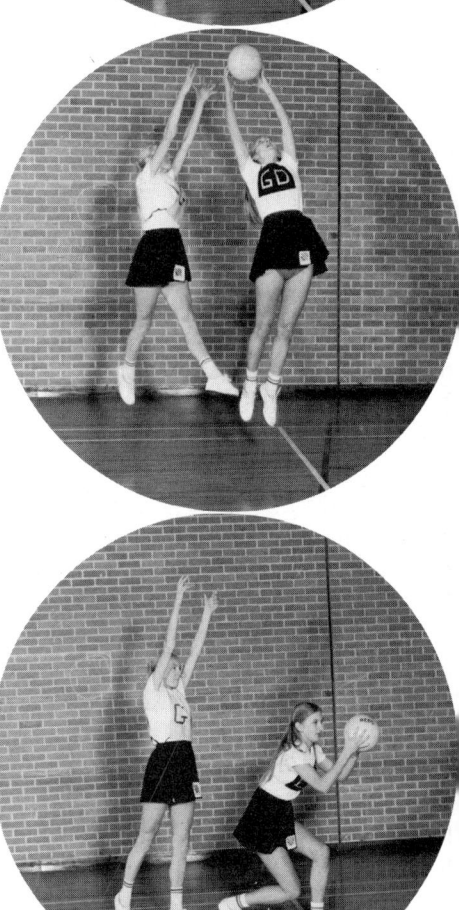

To intercept a lobbed pass, run back with your attacker once the ball leaves the thrower's hands. Avoid running backwards, run forwards with head turned to watch the ball, and time the leap to catch. When close marking an opponent who is standing her ground, watch the approaching ball to time your jump; adjust your position but be careful not to stand close in front of her, and back into her, thus making contact. Remain slightly to one side and slightly turned so that you can see both her and the oncoming ball; bend your knees in preparation and use your arms to get the utmost elevation to meet the ball as it flies overhead.

Whenever you see the possibility of making an interception, you must come to a quick decision as to whether you have the space in which to do it, without contacting another player.

As a defender you must be able to concentrate on the job, and sustain your concentration for the duration of the game. You must also be patient and determined, and never give up.

▲ GK has no space in which to make a catch of this rebound from the goal; she is too close to her opponent GS and is forcing contact

GK has made her interception by turning her movement to meet the ball, while GS has failed to make a decisive move or show her intentions to her thrower

A clean interception by the Australian Centre with one arm stretched for extra reach

Practise against different opponents so that you can defend effectively against players using different attacking techniques. Study each opponent's play and find out her strengths and her favourite movements. Few players have a varied repertoire of movement patterns, so try and recognise and anticipate what she will do when she comes into the attacking pattern of her team. Find out with which player she particularly combines. When defending, every player in the team must understand the Rules concerned with personal contact, contact with the ball, obstruction and interception.

Contact between the players in their attempt to reach the ball. The Umpire must decide whether both are equally to blame or whether the back player carries responsibility for reaching over the head of her opponent

You must also understand about the responsibility for contact when two opponents collide or contact each other. You must be careful not to stand so close to your opponent that her slightest movement results in contact; you must not throw yourself into the air to intercept a high ball, if in the process you collide with her or fall on her. The penalty is a Penalty Pass against you.

Practices for Intercepting

1. Work in threes. Two players pass the ball backwards and forwards, the third player attempts to intercept. Limit the space in which the two players dodge and allow the interceptor time to get into position for each throw. Try intercepting first the pass to the catcher, then the pass from the thrower.

While receiving the ball and keeping it away from her opponent, GS is watching the space she has to ground her right foot in relation to the goal line, the post and her opponent. GK is assessing her distance from GS's left foot

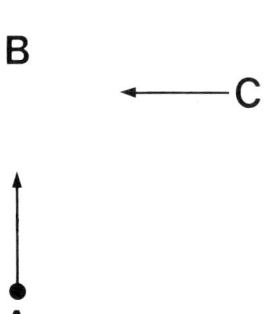

2. A with the ball passes to B; C waiting ten or more feet (3.05 m) away to the side runs when the ball leaves A's hands to intercept the pass.

3. Three against three. Concentrate on close marking, intercepting, moving in front of the opponent to intercept her throw.

4. In threes—two players lob pass; defender runs back, watching the ball, and tries to intercept.

Intercepting a Shot at Goal

As soon as a shooter has received the ball in the circle, the defender must make herself aware of the shooter's catching footwork, and, while quickly moving round to take up a position, carefully gauge the correct three feet (0.9 m) distance.

With the arms held low, take up a crouched position in front and slightly to the throwing side of the shooter. Watch her aim and time your jump forward and up to snatch the ball as soon as it leaves the shooter's hands. The forwardness of the jump will take you past the shooter and to the side of her, so that contact with her is not made.

Having taken her aim, the shooter will lower the ball preparatory to pushing it up towards the ring. Some

Intercepting a shot at goal

defenders watch the ball while others find it easier to watch the point of the elbow, and time the jump as the elbow is lowered.

The jump must be made, that is to say the defender must leave the ground, before the ball is pushed. The ball weighs one pound and therefore flies quickly from the shooter's hand, whereas the defender has to lift her body-weight, which even if only a hundred pounds, gives a sluggish lift. You must therefore jump early in order to be above the ball as it rises, and shoot your hands forward to a point just above the height at which the ball leaves the hands.

(a) Crouched ready for a spring ... which (b) is made slightly too late to effect an interception. (c) Avoiding contact after landing from the jump

(a)

(b)

(c)

Defender jumping to intercept the shot. Her jump is too early and, perhaps, too vertical

Inaccurate timing ruined this interception, the ball having passed overhead before the defender reached ◀

Timing is the most difficult aspect of the action. Untrained and unpractised defenders tend to mirror the shooter's action. Thus, as the shooter dips, the defender dips too in preparation and the ball and jumper rise together, which means that the ball has risen and passed over the defender before she reaches the full height of her jump and reach.

If you jump vertically from your position three feet (0.9 m) away, the ball will have risen too high for you to take it.

A few defenders like to make their attempt from a position to one side of the shooter, facing across her to avoid contact and reaching up with one hand to flick the ball away.

Should you make your jump too early and land closer than three feet (0.9 m), you will not be penalised for obstruction, if you quickly move out of the way or crouch in order not to affect the shooter's action.

Before you make your jump beware of taking a small step forward which puts you within three feet (0.9 m) of the shooter, or you will be penalised for obstruction. Be careful also not to raise your arm as you run round her to take up your position.

A close study should be made of the various shooting techniques, because obviously, a shooter will try to take evasive action to outwit your attempts to intercept. If she steps back from you, using her stepping foot to do so, and perhaps lifting her pivoting foot, remember that you cannot follow her, for your distance is measured from the place on the ground arrived at by the first grounded foot, whether she later lifts it or not. Your jump must therefore contain a greater forward element.

If the shooter steps to her right in a cross-over step with her left foot and pivots to face the goal and shoot, the action will have taken her forward as well as sideways from her original landing place. There is therefore no need for you to back away from her; step suddenly out directly sideways, having anticipated her movement. She will be nearer than three feet (0.9 m), but since she has stepped towards you, you are still free to raise your arms and make your intercepting move. Should you delay your move until she has committed herself to her movement, you will be responsible for any contact which occurs. Interception of the shot is an advanced skill, so if you do not possess the skill then defend the shooter or the ball.

GD's defending position is ineffective, especially if the shooter steps back, because she will not be able to jump in time to spoil the shot

Defending the Shooter

Place yourself between the shooter and the goal as for interception of the shot, watching the position of your feet, or your front foot if your weight is taken on one; stretch your arm so that your hand covers the ball but about six inches (15 cm) above it. Make a jump to try and keep the hand along the ball's flight. With arm held high, this is not a satisfactory starting position for a leap to intercept the ball. Neither must it be a distracting position, whereby you swing your arms across the shooter or towards her face, for these are termed intimidatory and could earn a penalty against you.

The object of this type of defending is to force the shooter to change her shooting techniques, so as to avoid the outstretched arm, or to hold the ball, or to pass.

Practices for Intercepting the Shot or Pass

1. A player A with a ball stands facing a wall or netting or a ten to twelve feet (3–3.5 m) goal

Defending—facing the opponent

area marked by two posts (Hockey goal). I, the Interceptor, places herself, at first, just in front of the wall, and later three to four feet (0.9-1.2 m) from A. A uses a variety of passes to attempt to hit the wall within the limited area. I tries to intercept the passes and prevent a hit being scored. Both players can move to catch the rebound.

2. A player A with the ball stands in the goal circle and her opponent B takes up her position in front to intercept. A holds the ball in her right hand stretched up above her right shoulder. B jumps to snatch the ball from A's hands, without contacting her.

3. Progress to A holding the ball in her aiming position above her head, then bending and straightening her elbows, so that B can learn to time her jump and gauge the place to aim her arm thrust. (The ball remains in A's possession.) Finally A aims and shoots without trying to avoid the interception.

Defending Players without the Ball

Facing the Opponent— Between Her and the Ball

This is a matter for each individual defender to decide. By turning her back to the ball, a defender has an easier task in following closely the movements of her opponent, but must turn suddenly to make her catch. She must get her cue from her opponent. If she is watching the flight of the ball, her eyes will give her away. Practise by getting a partner to throw the ball to your catching opponent and at your back, to left or right or above you. The partner can give directions as she passes the ball, to assist the defender to make the correct response.

Defending—between the player and the area she wishes to reach. This method of defending delays the opponent's attacking move, but does not lead to possession of the ball

Behind the Opponent— Between Her and Her Goal

If caught out of position and unable to make an attempt to intercept the flying ball, you can drop back, face your opponent and guard the area into which she wishes to come to play an active part in team attack. As Goal Defence, take up your stance just outside the goal circle and attempt to keep your opposing Goal Attack out of the circle. The action will not get you the ball, but you can upset your opponent's timing and the rhythm of the opposing team's attack. Similarly Wing Attack's movement to reach the goal third can be slowed. This method of defence should not be overdone; it is a delaying action; the attacking team has no difficulty in keeping possession of the ball. The aim of the defending team is to gain possession of the ball, the only means by which they can score.
The defender must be extremely careful not to make contact with her opponent, as the latter dodges to move past to reach her goal.

Good positioning by GK and GD, but poor backing up by GA and GS. Here GS was forced to stand behind GK, too far back

Defending the Goal

When one of the two shooters receives the ball in the goal circle, and finds herself in such a position that she is doubtful of scoring the goal, she must consider quickly whether to attempt the shot or pass the ball to her partner, if the latter is available and nearer the post. If she decides to shoot, her partner must receive the cue and move quickly to stand where she can catch the rebound if the shot is missed. GA is taking the shot. Then GS places herself just inside the Goal Line on the opposite side of the post and a good step away from it to retrieve the 'over-shot'.

Her opponent GK then has three alternatives—to stand in front of GS in a position under the ring from which she is able to retrieve only the ball which passes through the ring; or to stand behind or to the right of GS, both second-best places. Whichever of the two players positions herself first, gains the advantage.

GA must follow up her shot—

Good catching of the rebound from GA's shot

she should know by the 'feel of her throw', the result of the shot. Her opponent already positioned between GA and the post should usually hold the initiative.

In the photograph on page 77, GA has made the shot and failed to move in. GK gained her best position first, while GS has been forced to stand behind her. Therefore both attacking players are out of position and fail to retrieve the ball.

It is a mistake for all four players to jump together for the ball, or for either partnership to do so.

The throw up

The Throw Up

The throw up is an individual skill which, if practised assiduously, can quicken your reaction time whenever you have to make a rapid response to any signal.

The throw up is awarded whenever two opponents catch the ball simultaneously while attempting to gain possession of the ball, simultaneously enter an offside area, knock the ball out of court, or contact each other.

The two opponents involved stand facing one another, and facing their own goal. The Umpire stands facing the centre point between the players' feet and holds the ball on the palm of her hand between them at a level which is below the shoulders of the shorter player when in a normal standing position. Each may assume any stance. The arms, however,

Winning at the throw up

must be straight and against the sides of the body, and there must be a distance of three feet (0.9 m) between the nearer foot of each player. The Umpire blows her whistle and at the same time tosses the ball not more than two feet (0.6 m) into the air.
Each player must be motionless, without any sway forwards, concentrating her attention on the ball and the sound of the whistle.
The ball should be taken as early as possible and while it is rising from the Umpire's hands.

Having trapped the ball, continue the swing of the arms and ball over your shoulder and away from your opponent.

Practice

Player A with the ball gives a throw up between B and C; E on B's team and F in C's team stand by marking each other. If B takes the ball, then E gets free and receives a pass, and throws to stationary player D. D gives a throw up between E and F. If F gets it, C gets free and receives the pass, and throws back to A.

```
        A
B       •       C

       E F

        D
```

Strategy—Team Attack

The play of all competitive team games is a complex skill, in which the individual contribution made by each player is harnessed to the skill of the other members of the team. Each player's action, whether it be passing or attacking, affects what comes next, e.g. A makes a move, B replies, A replies to that reply, etc. This provides a variability with which the learner cannot cope. It is the task of the coach to split up the elements of the game which are highly interdependent.

The elements of team play can be provided for at the beginner stage by the careful organisation of practice situations for the teaching of the basic skills contained within 'passing the ball'.

It was recommended that when teaching the **how** of throwing, attacking, shooting and defending as basic skills, then drills, divorced from the game itself, can be used, where the player is solely concerned with the building up of her own individual movement patterns. The later practice of **when** and **where** of each skill is best organised in game situations, e.g. 'Passing in twos', first without and then against opposition. Now the player is confronted with problems. She must predict when and where the ball will arrive, she must select the appropriate throw and predict when to launch the ball and where she must aim her pass. When a third player is introduced to a team of two, each is faced by yet another problem—choice of player to use. Unpredictable variability is the hardest of all things to cope with.

Given the problems confronting players learning a team game, it is clear that fourteen players are unable to play a full game without going through the gradual stages of build up, from individual play to two in a team, three in a team and so on, together with a gradual build up of a knowledge of the Rules of the Game.

Principles of Team Attack Play

The general principles of team attack play can be taught in groups of three versus three. These principles are:
1. That a team in possession of the ball is the attacking team.
2. That by using their skills within the framework of the Rules a team aims to move the ball from wherever it was gained to the goal and score,

WA receiving the ball in the attacking goal third from C in centre third. C follows up after her throw

against opposition.

3. That a team not in possession of the ball is the defending team, and their object is to gain possession and so put the team in a position to score.

4. That a team consists of a division of players each with a particular function and each with a limited area of the court in which to operate. The playing position of each player denotes both the area in which she operates and the part she plays in team attack.

Wing Attack, Goal Attack and Goal Shooter form the 'front line' of the attack; they operate mainly in the attacking goal third of the court, and by Rule must be in that goal third for the start of the game and the restart after each goal. Goal Attack and Goal Shooter are the only two allowed in the goal circle and they are responsible for making the attempts to score and must be entirely within the circle to make the the attempt.

Wing Attack, allowed to play in the centre third but whose main operational area is the goal third, is the player mainly responsible for feeding the ball to her two shooters.

Attack move up court with main attacking players in the goal third and WD moving the ball forward.
As a coach, you can see in this picture the two good options open to WD

Wing Defence, Goal Defence and Goal Keeper operate mainly in the defending goal third, only Goal Defence and Goal Keeper being allowed in the goal circle. It is they who initiate a team attack if their opposing shooters miss their attempt to score and the ball is sent out of court, or the defenders intercept the ball from the rebound. Together with Wing Defence, these three players are mainly responsible for moving the ball away from the circle through the defending goal third and into the centre third. Centre is the pivot of the team, able to operate in all three thirds, but not in the goal circles. She starts the game and restarts it after a goal from the centre circle, she and her opponent being the only players allowed in the centre third at these times. Her principal function is to link the attacking play by the defenders to that of the three attackers, while she can assist both groups of players in the goal thirds.

This organisation of the game gives the coach areas of work which should be sorted out, taught and practised so that out of chaos disciplined play can emerge.

The areas of work to be coached can be separated into the main situations which arise in team attack:
1. Attack play from the **centre pass** to score.
2. Attack play from a **throw in** behind the defending goal circle, or an interception by the defenders inside the goal circle.
3. Attack play from a **throw in** behind the side lines bounding the defending centre or attacking thirds of the court, or from behind the goal line bounding the attacking goal circle.
4. Attack play from a **penalty** awarded in any area.
5. **Circle** play.

Basic Systems

The coach should plan simple basic systems of attack to help players understand how to play as a team rather than as seven individuals. Systematic play can be devised to deal with the main situations outlined above. Systems of passing in attack require a basic understanding and practice of:
- passing ahead of a moving player
- timing a pass
- holding the run
- timing the move to receive a pass
- footwork
- co-operation with two other players.

With this skills equipment, the teaching of systematic play affords training in the application of skills.

Basic systems of play serve only as a vehicle for the understanding of the principles of attack. The use of only one system of attack play either for half-court or full-court attack could be broken by a discerning defending team. An established team must be equipped with alternative plans according to their knowledge of the strengths and weaknesses of each member of their own team and of the defence system of the opposing team. There are several stages in the planning of systems of play:

1. Plan the path of the ball to the goal

The most direct path from one end of the court to the other is a simple straight line to the goal down the middle of the court, or one travelling between the middle and either side line. One must remember, however, that a straight line too near the side lines is risky since the ball is easily lost out of court, by an inaccurate pass, or a fumbled catch.

2. Plan the moves of the players:

- the order in which they enter the attack
- the direction for each player to move to her catching point
- the starting position of each player and her preliminary move to join the attack
- the subsequent move of each player after she has caught and thrown the ball, in order to move forward in support and drop back in defence.

All players must know when to enter the attack and where and when to move. It saves a cluttering of players in an area of the court, especially the

WA (arrowed) is in the defending half of the court, thus muddling her WD

centre court in which ten players in a game could congregate. It saves energy to make one maximum effort. It trains players in the use of space, in understanding their main operational area, and gives every player in the team opportunity to practise their basic skills. In an elementary game a team tends to avoid using the weak players and overwork the strong members of a team, whereas it is the weak ones who require the practice.

The few simple systems form the basis of all attacking moves.

Half-Court Systems

Half-Court Systems from the Centre Pass to Score

Although it is possible to make a two-pass attack on the goal it requires great skill to bring it off. A three-pass attack is ideal; the greater the number of passes used, the greater is the opportunity for the defenders to break the attack.

By rule the centre pass must be received (or touched) in the centre third. To move the ball towards the goal, the second pass is caught in the goal third and the third in the goal circle. GD, WD, WA and GA are able to move into the centre third to receive the centre pass. If all four make a move to take the ball, this leaves only GS in an attacking position. In general, if WA is selected then either shooter is free to take the second pass, and the second shooter free to receive the ball in the circle.

Earlier it was said that the attack play through the team's attacking half of the court is mainly borne by Centre, Wing Attack, Goal Attack and Goal Shooter so the first system taught should follow up this statement.

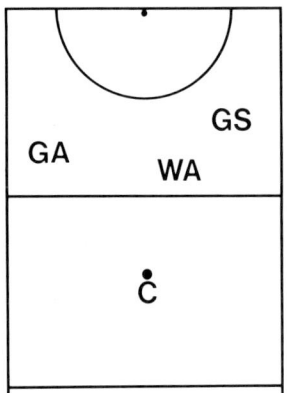

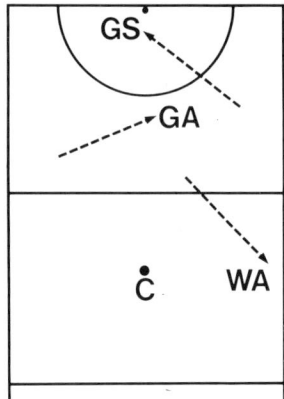

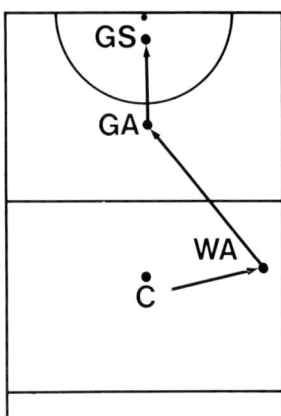

Half-Court Systems of Attack Play from the Centre Pass: Learning Stages

1. Starting places

WA, GA, GS are positioned in the goal third, from which each can make her run to receive the ball.
C holds the ball in the centre circle.
Leave out opponents, so that players can concentrate on time and space.

2. Order of passes—direction of moves

WA moves out to the side of the centre third; on arrival C passes her the ball.
GA moves across to the middle of the goal third; she receives the pass from WA.
GS moves into the goal circle and towards the goal; she receives the pass from GA and scores.

3. Timing of moves

WA makes her move on the starting whistle. C passes after assessing WA's direction and speed.
GA holds her run until WA has control of the ball and has turned to face goal third, ready to throw.
GS holds her run until GA is ready to throw.

(a) Start of play. C has the ball in the centre circle while the attacking players and their opponents are in the goal third. (b) WA moves out to the side, receives from C and passes (c) to GA in the goal third. (d) GS receives from GA and scores

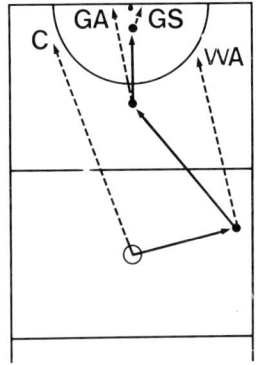

4. Follow up by each player after her throw

C to edge of goal circle via the free side of the goal third.
WA through her free side of the goal third.
GA to the opposite side of the goal post away from GS to catch the rebounded shot.
GS to the post to catch rebound.
Each of these players must make themselves available for a second pass.

5. Moves against opposition

The Centre's position at the line up is fixed. She must stand within the centre circle; Wing Attack is free to take any place in the goal third and is free to move but should move rapidly on the whistle into the centre third.

Since the attacking team holds the initiative, Wing Attack must get what advantage she can from her opponent.
(a) Both WA and GA, by placing themselves close to the sides of the transverse line, invite their respective opponents to defend them on the court side, thus limiting the effectiveness of their manoeuvres to receive the pass, and playing into their hands.
(b) The nearer to the centre of the line WA places herself, the more difficult she is to defend. She has space in which to

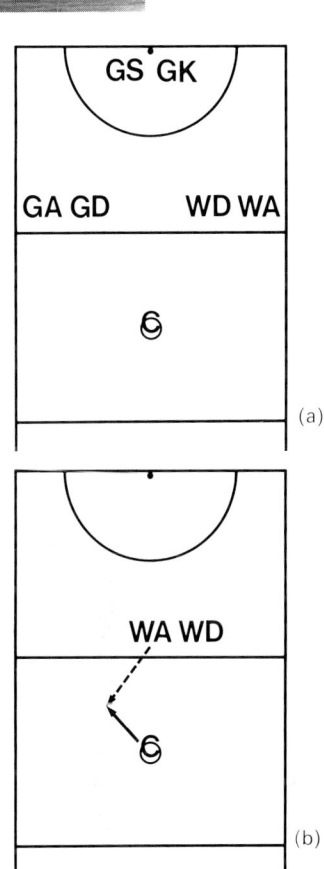

Attacking play in the attacking goal third. Having received the ball from the centre third, WA is preparing to pass to GA free from the attentions of her opponent. There is obvious co-operation between the two — witness GA's run, diagonally across court towards the thrower

move, out to left or right, whichever is her undefended side.

GA, taking the second pass, has a greater problem. She must be careful that she does not inhibit her WA's move by moving into her space and taking her opponent with her. She must assist her WA by keeping her own opponent occupied in defending her. There is no ruling that GS, GA and WA must line up as in (a), or that they must be stationary. Players should be encouraged to discuss among themselves and try out different placings and relationships according to the half-court strategy they will employ at each centre pass. The 'line up' is a team tactical situation, in which the Centre should play a leading role. When the players have understood the basic principles of team passing, and have practised a simple basic system of attack play from the centre, then the problems relating to positioning posed by the defence should be discussed by the coach with the players. The coach should set problems for the players to answer, for no strategy can succeed unless the players themselves are trained to solve each problem posed by the opposition. As was said before, there are so many variables within one situation of the game that one must clarify and simplify first, and build up from simple beginnings which are definite and follow certain principles.

Alternative Centre Pass Strategy in a Three-Pass Attack

The three attacking players, WA, GA and GS, can be used in a different order to that already shown, still using each player once only:

1. WA—GA—GS, i.e. centre third, goal third, circle
2. WA—GS—GA
3. GA—WA—GS

When the players have understood and learnt these basic attacking moves, many other variations can be planned by the attacking members of the team using different patterns of play to move the ball from the centre to the goal, and taking advantage of the special abilities of each player, and the comparative strength of the defenders.

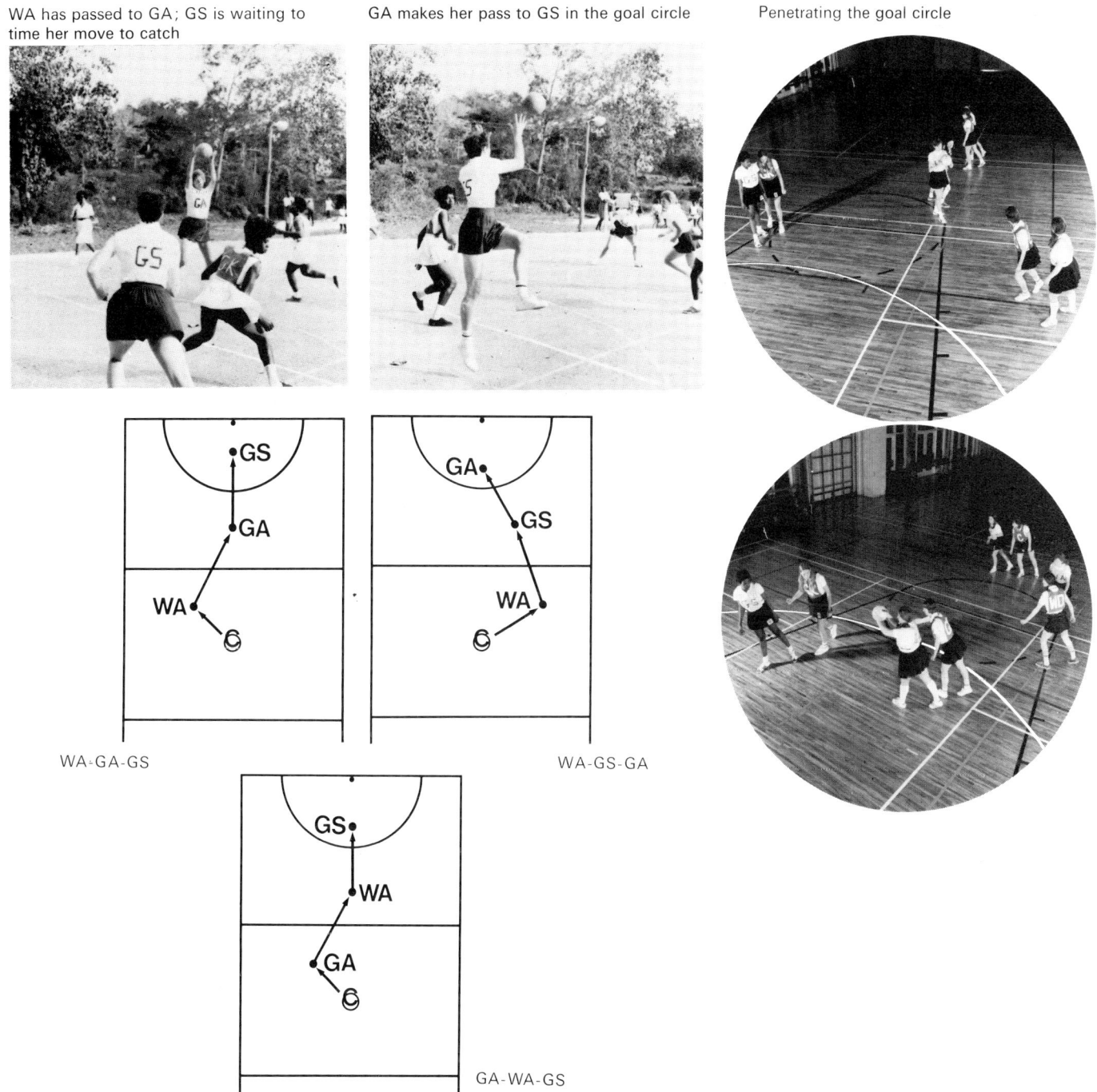

Centre pass to GD moving into attacking half of the court

Penetration into the circle from a point in the goal third at the front of the circle is more easily made than from the side, because of the wide-angled arc offered to the thrower. The player used in the goal third should try and make for the position shown in (1) rather than (2).

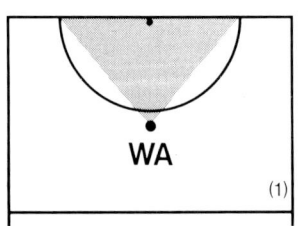

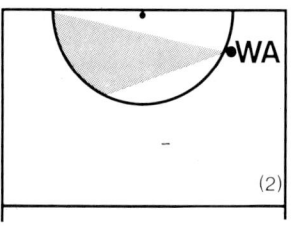

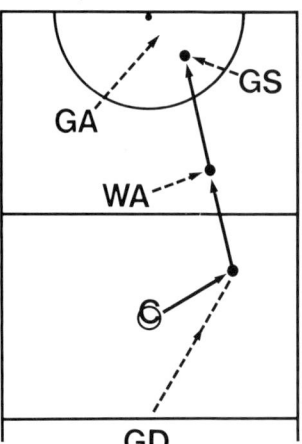

Should WA, GA and GS be under pressure, then C can use WD or GD for the centre pass giving WA and GA the use of the goal third.

WD and GD should try to receive the centre pass as far forward into the centre third as possible so that the ball can be moved by Centre towards the goal.

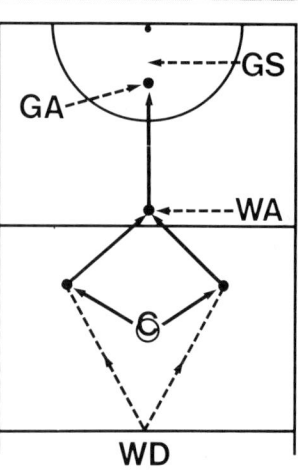

By taking the initiative in positioning in the defending goal third, and making use of her free side, WD can cross to the right of the C or run straight forward, to ensure that her opponent is not marking her on the ball side, and so strive for an interception.

Centre pass to WD. GA in front of WD moves to the left. WA prepares to move out to the right to split the defence. GS free in circle

Repositioning

When each player involved in moving the ball from the centre pass to the goal circle has made her pass, she must move forward to support the rest of the attacking players, to make herself available for a second pass.

C to edge of the circle, travelling through the empty area of play.

WA to edge of circle on the opposite side to C.

GA to the post.

Having learnt and practised attacking plans using WA, GA, WD and GD for the first pass with success, the team is faced with the problem of how Centre and the rest of the team are to communicate which of these plans is to be used in the match. Some teams decide before the match by fixing an order in which players take the first pass. This could lead to the possible waste of a pass if Centre discovers that she is unable to use GA, for example, because of her opponent's superiority in the particular situation.

Some teams get over this problem by using a system of signals by means of which the Centre, Captain or circle player tells her team which player is to be used at each centre pass. This can be successful if the signaller is an intelligent and observant player.

There is always the danger in teaching systematic play that the system as planned becomes the end product. I must stress again that planned moves serve as a basis for learning and understanding the principles of attack or defence.

Against a better team, a plan which is repeated unvaryingly will be recognised and countered by the opposition. The attackers then have no alternative reply. Any attack is only as good as the sum of the skill of each individual taking part.

Full-Court Systems

When a team fails to net the ball from a shot at goal, and the ball passes out of court behind the goal line, the team defending at the shot is awarded a throw in from behind the goal line. It is now the team in possession of the ball, and therefore the attacking team, which has a chance of scoring if the ball can be moved through the court to their scoring circle.

Deciding among the variable possibilities in moving the ball forward by seven players with

GK and GD moving the ball away from their opponents' shooting circle to attack

Attack play at the defending end of the court—WD with the ball and GD breaking out of the circle to receive

area limitations which also vary in extent for each playing position, against opposition which can also be varied, presents a difficult and frightening task to the inexperienced coach.

As the individual skills are isolated from the game, presented in their simplest form at first and then developed through carefully planned stages, so the techniques of team offensive and defensive play must be analysed and broken down into simple components, which are easily understood by beginners, and then developed again through carefully planned stages.

A full-court system is an extension of the half-court system described for use at the centre pass to score. A three-pass attack was presented using the three principal front-line attackers, Wing Attack, Goal Attack and Goal Shooter, from the centre circle. From a throw in from behind the goal line of the defending third, the attack is started and the ball moved through the defending goal third by Goal Keeper, Goal Defence and Wing Defence, passed on to Centre and the attack is then passed to the three attacking players. The stages of learning follow, as for half-court:

- positioning before the start of the attack
- shape of attack or pattern of ball flight
- order of passes
- timing of moves
- repositioning.

Stage 1. Learning Drills for a Full-Court System:
- direction of attack
- pattern—straight line up the middle of the court
- order of Play—GK—GD—WD—C—WA—GA—GS
- positioning—above order spaced down the side line.

1. GK holds the ball.
2. GD sprints across court towards opposite side line.
3. GK aims her pass so that GD takes it on the pattern line.
4. GD catches the ball on the run, lands and pivots to face WD and is ready to throw.
5. This action of readiness to throw serves as a cue for WD to make her sprint across to receive the pass on the pattern line.
6. Continue with same cue to start the sprint, thus moving the ball on to C, WA, GA and GS, who scores the goal.

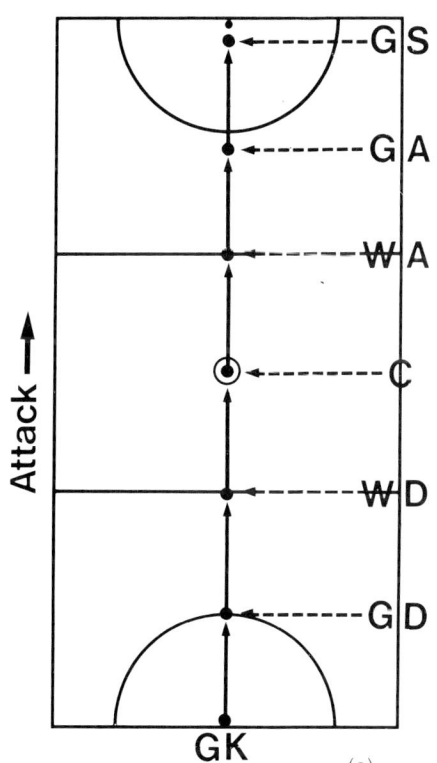

(a)

The opposing team can practise their attack at the same time starting with GK at the opposite end of the court, and her team players lined up at the opposite side of the court. This team skill is based on the skill of passing between two players and is development of practices on page 39 under 'Throwing Skills', dealing with timing and direction of both throwing and receiving a pass. Competition can be introduced between the two teams:
1. The team wins who can carry out this manoeuvre with accuracy, using a stated type of throw, accuracy of pattern and footwork, without dropping the ball, and throwing so that the catcher must be fully stretched in order to make her catch.
2. The team wins which scores the goal first.

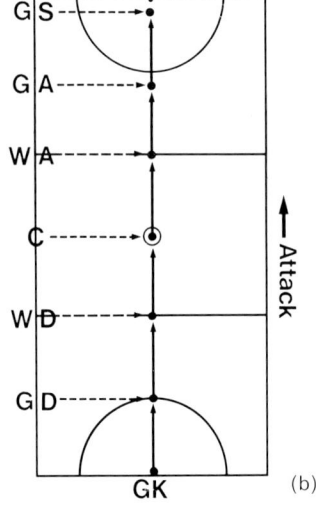

(b)

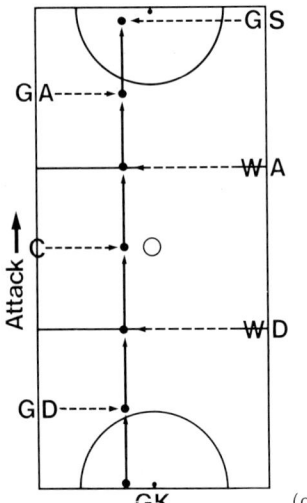

(c)

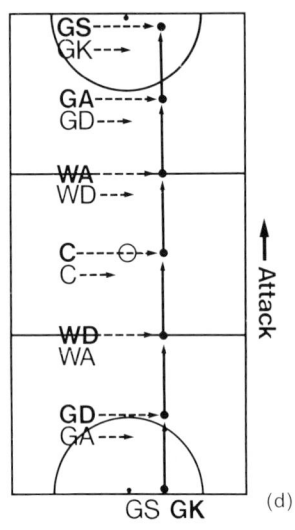

(d)

Repeat the drill from a positioning at the left-hand side line. Each runner often finds it more difficult to thrust out the right leg and left arm to make her catch safe, and her footwork correct on a pass from her right, and a pivot quarter-turn to the left to make her throw. (Fig. b.)

Repeat the drill, each successive player positioning herself on opposite sides of the court. (Fig. c.)

Bring in opposition

Each player now has her opponent positioned between herself and the ball. She must therefore use her attacking techniques to free herself and run to her left on to the straight line pattern to receive the pass. (Fig. d.)

Repeat in the opposite direction. Insist that every attacker uses a stated technique as taught, thus building up a vocabulary of skills. Having scored the goal, the opposing GK starts her attack in the opposite direction.

In each of the team skills (a), (b), (c) and (d) introduce repositioning by each player. After moving across the court to make her catch, complete the throw and continue running on in the same direction.

Practice (d) is obviously a great advance on the earlier practices, which trained an awareness of space and timing. Now there must be an increased understanding and co-operation by any one player to assist the thrower in making a successful pass and to make a successful pass herself using the assistance of the receiver. The training of players in units of three is the very essence of team play in netball. It is part of the nature of a schoolgirl

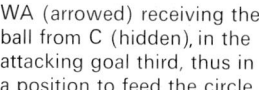
WA (arrowed) receiving the ball from C (hidden), in the attacking goal third, thus in a position to feed the circle

put into a full game of netball too early to demand the ball and then to throw it to a friend who can be trusted to catch the ball and return it. The slow learners and poor movers are left out of the play, or blamed if they throw the ball away. The learning of disciplined team play involves character education, and the shaping of proper attitudes. Team plays are rich in opportunities to teach honesty, player consideration, team spirit, sportsmanship and other valued concepts.
Full-court attacking skills should now be applied in a game situation.

Starting Positions in the Game Situation

Order of play

GK—GD—WD = the team of three with the responsibility of moving the ball from the goal line, through the goal third and into the centre third, to reach C. C—WA—GA—GS through the attacking half of the court to GS in the shooting circle and so to score.
When 'play' is called all players in the team must position themselves in readiness to enter the attack sequence in their operational area (Diag. a, page 96.)

Pass 1. C should move away from the circle to give space for GD to move out of the circle to receive the first pass. WD draws her opponent out to the left. The first pass must be caught in the goal third.
Pass 2. WD moves diagonally forward towards the middle of the transverse line, i.e. towards the ball to receive the pass. GK moves forward and out to the right, while GD crosses to the left in support of WD.
Pass 3. C moves from the side line diagonally forward towards the centre circle. Meanwhile WA and GA retreat to clear the space for the C keeping to the

(a) Starting Positions

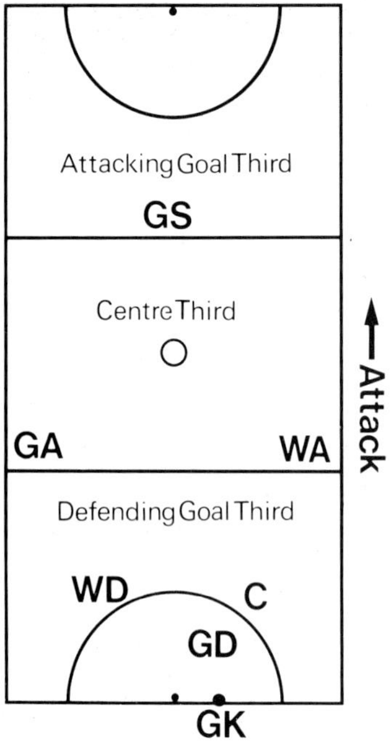

Attacking Goal Third
GS

Centre Third

GA   WA

Defending Goal Third

WD   C
   GD
   GK

← Attack

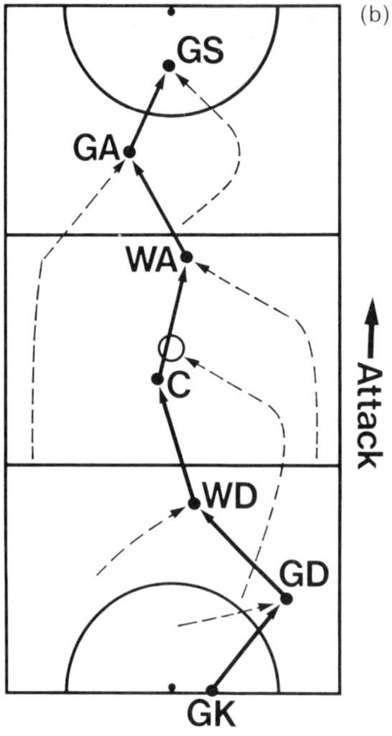

(b) Order of Play
Pattern of Passing
Positioning

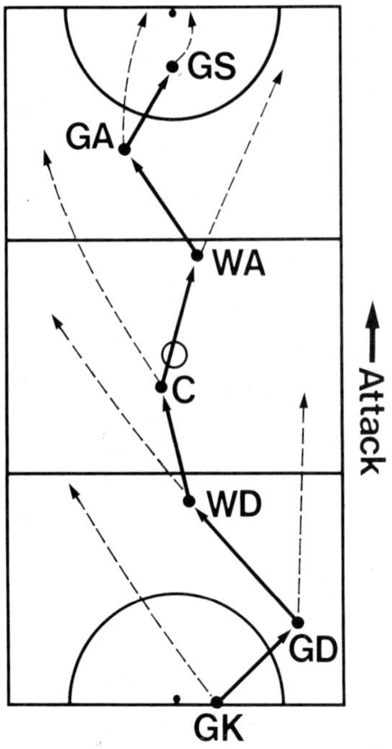

GS
GA
WA
C
WD
GD
GK

← Attack

side lines. WD follows up to the left.

Pass 4. WA moves diagonally forward and to the middle to receive her pass near the second transverse line. C moves forward and to the right where WA came from, to be ready to assist penetration of the goal circle.

Pass 5. GA from the side line, sights her goal and moves towards the circle to receive the pass. WA follows to the edge of the circle.

Pass 6. GS, from the right-hand side line, moves into the circle and receives the pass from GA near enough to the goal to be certain of scoring. GA moves to the post to take the rebound if GS fails to score. The above patterns of play and order of play serve as a basis for the understanding of the basic principles of attack play.

(c) Follow-up run after passing

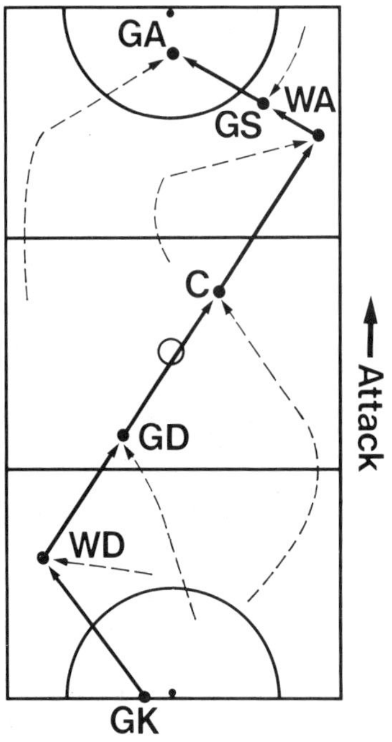

GS
GA
WA
C
WD
GD
GK

← Attack

(d) Alternative Patterns

GA
WA
GS
C
GD
WD
GK

← Attack

Same sequence with opposition. Notice positioning and direction of runs ▶

Sequence of passes up court; GK-GD-WD-C. Without opposition ▶

WD-C-WA-GA-GS

In the goal third and on her way into the circle, GA gathers the ball coming from her right and converts its flight into a throw into the goal circle. Centre moves across court to reposition herself

GK-WD-C

Alternative Orders of Play and Pattern

The players stationed in the goal third for the start of a full-court attack must now experiment and practise alternative orders to move the ball through the defending goal third. The possibilities are:

1. GK—WD—GD—C
2. GD—GK—WD—C
3. GD—WD—GK—C

C could be brought earlier into the attack, in which case WD should move into the centre third to take the later pass.

It is unwise for GD to move too far down into the centre third in case her team loses possession, and the ball swings quickly to the opponent's goal.

GD-GK-WD-C

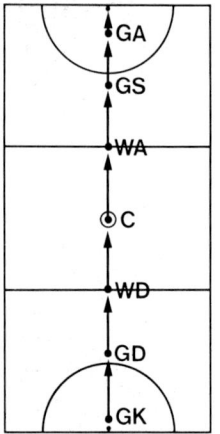

Straight Line Pattern

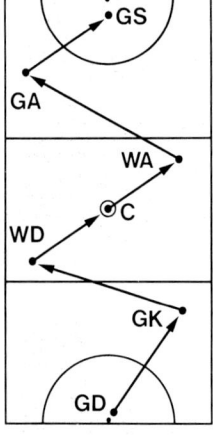

Zig Zag Pattern

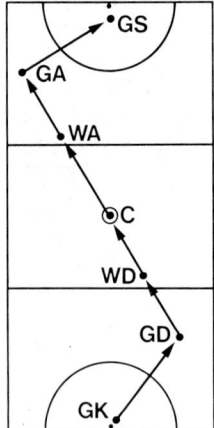

Diagonal or Z Pattern

GK ready to start the team attack. Anticipating a pass, GD (arrowed) has an opening out of the circle

Practise straight line patterns, diagonal or zigzag.
If the opposing team in possession of the ball loses that possession, the new attacking team must quickly change their role from defending to attacking. Depending on the area in which the change of possession takes place, the order and pattern is picked up from that place.
Should a penalty be awarded in the defending goal third then GD or WD should take it, unless time would be wasted in their moving to the spot. This allows the C and attacking three players to position themselves in a forward position.
If in the attacking half of the court, then C should take the pass.
The point is made that WA, GA and GS are needed to operate in the goal third and goal circle to bring the attacking movement to a successful conclusion.

GK throws in from the side-line of the goal third

GD has the ball while C has got free and is moving to draw the pass. WD is already running, but not to take the first pass; she is going for the best position in which to receive from C

From the goal third side-line WD passes to GD. C is positioning herself to take the next pass

Shooter breaking away in the circle ▶

Without a plan, each player is working as an individual and the game becomes undisciplined; the centre third becomes cluttered when GA and WA play in the defending half of the centre third while WD and GD play in the attacking half of the same third.

When the ball goes out of court at the defending third side lines, plan for GK or GD to take the throw in, depending upon the nearness to the opponent's goal circle. Pick up the order of play from that point, so that the defender not involved in throwing in can stay back to defend in case a mistake is made.

From the side lines of the centre third allow WD or C to take the throw in, while from the attacking third side lines, C or WA. It is unwise to allow GA or GS to take this throw in; they are needed to take the ball in the goal circle.

Basic Circle Play

A team attack at all levels of play often breaks down in the attacking goal third, because at this point the ball has to be aimed into the small area of the goal circle.

Goal Shooter and Goal Attack must develop the various attacking techniques to free themselves from close-marking opponents, and must be skilled in making sudden changes of direction within a small space, and be able to dodge and lunge to either side, or dodge and sprint to either side.

Although shooters need to practise shooting from all points in the circle, it is undoubtedly easier to score from shots made within the inner half of the goal circle, i.e. a distance of three to eight feet (0.9-2.5 m) away from the goal. Remember not to position yourself near the post with your back to it—you must be aware of its position all the time. This is the space in which to receive the pass.

Goal Shooter and Goal Attack must have a close understanding with each other and plan their tactical moves. The positioning of each player and the timing of the moment to enter the attack is difficult for these two players. While watching the progess of their team's attack up the court, there is always a tendency to over-anticipate and begin creeping into the circle, drawing the opponent with you.

Position yourselves on opposite sides of the goal circle, and watch the progress of your WA, with whom you will both work most closely.

Practices

1. WA—GS—GA

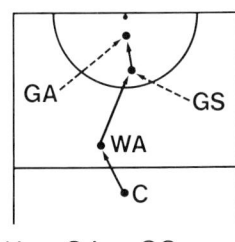

WA—GA—GS

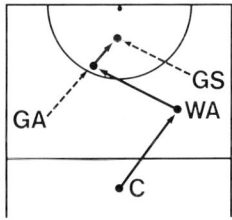

C with the ball throws to WA standing in goal third. WA selects the shooter in the better position to move for the pass. WA selects different parts of the goal third in which to receive and make her throw.
The first of the two shooters to receive the ball passes it on to the other, to score the goal, and moves to the post to get the rebound.

Add opponents.
2. C with ball, throws it to WA who passes into the free player in the circle. If neither free, she passes back to C who passes in. GA and GS must work together and be aware of each other's positions in the circle, so that both of you do not make for the same space at the same time.
If unable to pass in safely, WA and C must keep possession of the ball and manoeuvre themselves between the front of the circle and the sides, passing between them until the opening occurs—all four attacking players working hard. Try and avoid lobbing the ball in to the

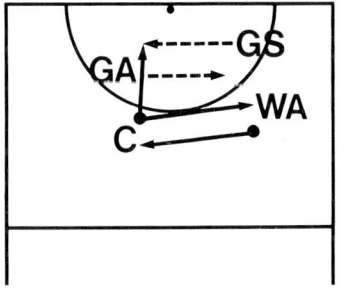

shooters, for defenders are often tall, and a lob has to be very well judged to succeed.
WA and C should keep close to the circle edge so that their opponents must move to the side to retreat to the three feet (0.9 m) distance when the catch is made.
A shooter who is forced by her opponent to run towards her thrower and therefore away from the goal, and catches the ball near the circle edge is faced with three problems:
- she must turn about to face her goal, and use her feet in the most advantageous way to do so
- she is faced with a long shot
- her opponent is already between her and the goal with a greater chance to intercept the shot.

In answer to these problems she has two alternatives—to risk a shot or to pass.
With a close understanding, together with a grasp of the sense of anticipation and a

▲ Defence out-positioned

Scoring the goal

quick reaction, the two shooters can outwit the defenders and move the ball between them to gain a shooting position nearer the post. WA and C, too, must also be alert for a pass, to allow both shooters to reposition themselves. Possession of the ball must be maintained until the goal is scored.

The attacking effort must not cease until the ball passes through the ring. Since the scoring average of teams is rarely higher than 60 per cent of attempts, both shooters must 'back up' each shot and try and make a catch from the rebound. Work together to position yourselves so that you have space in which to jump. Watch the ball on its flight and anticipate the angle at which it will drop. Time your jump to reach the ball at the highest possible point.

Remember that with the change of rules a shooter who shoots for goal and fails to hit the ring or post cannot catch the ball again until one of the opposition has touched it.

Strategy—Team Defence

Man-to-Man Defence

The team which has possession of the ball holds the initiative, and is in the strategical position to score. It must therefore be the first aim of the defending team to halt the attack by gaining possession of the ball. The responsibility lies with all seven players of that team. Throughout a match each player is constantly alternating between attacking and defending. The attitude of each of two opposing players changes. As attacker you free yourself, you move away; as defender you guard, you close the space. In netball it is easier to attack, and harder to defend. Every player in the team must assume responsibility for her own opponent, and practise both attacking skills and defending skills regardless of what their playing position is in the team.

The qualities required of a player whether attacking or defending are fundamentally the same:
1. The ability to concentrate on the game for the duration of each period of play.
2. An awareness of each other on court.
3. The ability to make split-second decisions.
4. The development of peripheral vision, the ability to see a widespread view of the court, the movement of players and the flight of the ball, as well as focusing attention on your opponent or the ball.

Defending requires in addition a determination not to give up trying, and not to give way or collapse under pressure.

In the beginning stages of a match, try and assess your opponent's play. Discover:

1. Where she positions herself at the start of play; this is particularly necessary for a WD, GD and GK. By her position and alertness, is she going to be used for the centre pass?
2. What techniques does she use to get free?
3. Is her ball-handling sure? Can she take a pass from both sides?
4. Has the attacking team a plan of attack for the centre pass?
5. Is GA used in the centre third? Then close mark her on her goal side to delay her entry into the shooting circle.
6. Does the GS remain in the circle standing her ground? If so, do not stand still, but keep on the move, side to side between her and the ball, with sufficient room to enable you to manoeuvre. Never allow her to get so close to you as to

GK is marking to intercept the ball while GD is trying to slow her opponent's run into the circle

GK and GS working well together. GK makes use of her height and spring to intercept the pass from GS to GA

prevent you from moving in any direction.

7. Do both shooters leave the circle at the same time to help in the attack? If so, you have one of two alternatives:

- to continue to close-mark her so that the player with the ball dare not risk a pass to her, or makes an error in passing so that you can make an interception and gain the ball
- to retire to the edge of the circle to cut off her path into the circle, which can delay her entry. You must realise that this will not get you the ball. Your opponent is a free player and can play the ball and keep possession until she can find an opening.

8. Does your opponent position herself at the side of the court? If so, position yourself on the court side of her.

Keep alert and adjust your position as you watch the attack proceeding up court and can assess the probable direction and timing of her move into the attack.

A defender finds it much easier to shadow the attacker who stands still, and much harder to cover the player constantly on the move.

▲ GD is waiting at the edge of the circle prepared to defend GA and delay her entry into it

GK is poised to help her partner if neither GD nor her opponent is able to make a clean catch ▶

Conversely, it is easier for an attacker to be constantly on the move and keep her defender guessing.

To defend your opponent's throw, you must accustom yourself to be aware of your opponent's landing foot in order to keep within the rule which allows you to defend the throw only when you are three feet (0.9 m) or more away from the landing foot. If in doubt as to the landing, give yourself a margin for error. Keep your arms down until you have arrived, then spread your arms wide and high to form a screen. Watch the ball and try and launch yourself into its path as you recognise the type of pass being made. If it fails, close mark again.

WD and C

When the attack reaches the goal circle WD and C must continue to mark their opponents. If C and WA tend to move round to the corners, then mark them on the outer side. Be alert for a pass out by the shooters, and for the loose balls.

GD and GK

When your opponent receives the ball study her footwork. You must be particularly careful not to obstruct her by making a defensive move within three feet (0.9 m)—it will earn her a penalty pass or shot for goal which *you* are not allowed to defend. GD and GK must work as a team; be prepared to switch roles if your partner is in difficulty.

According to your opponent's position within the circle decide whether it is better to attempt to intercept her shot or defend her so that she has to alter her shot.

In preparing for a missed shot, be sure you are not too close to the post and boxed in.

Zone Defence

A defending team can set up a zone defence manoeuvre to counter a fast-moving attack. With this type of defending tactic, the players leave their opponents and fall back to defend an area of the court. They disregard the opposing players and watch the ball; their action is similar to that of a football goal keeper. Watch his positioning in the goal mouth and see how he adjusts it according to the angle of the shot to the goal line.

A zone can be set up in the centre third or the opposing team's attacking goal third. The players taking part in the manoeuvre must between them cover the attacking area both in width and depth.

Zone defence

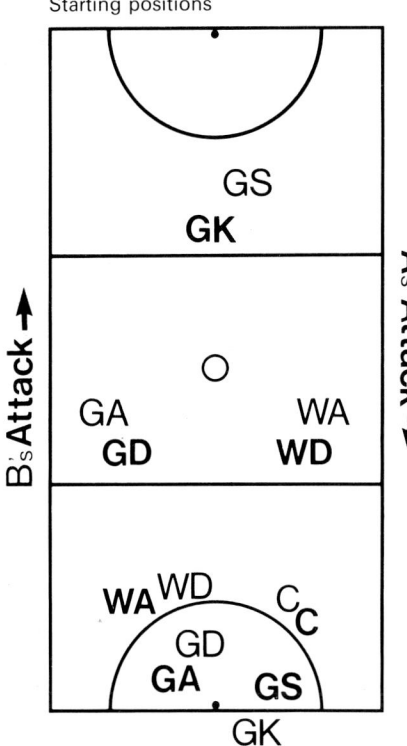

The two main centre third zoning players move sideways together being careful that the space between them does not widen and allow a pass through between them. They both move towards the side at which the thrower catches the ball as early as possible:

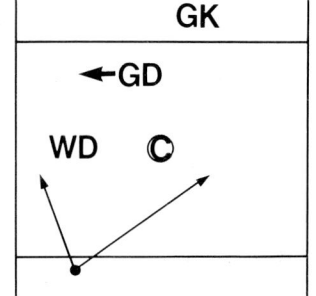

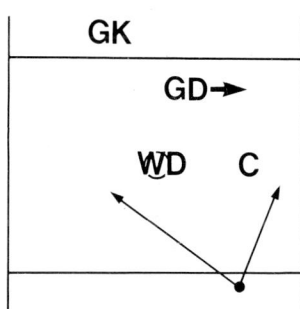

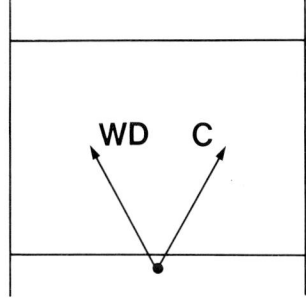

Example 1

The GS of attacking team A has missed her shot and the ball has gone out of court behind the goal line. Team A is now the defending team. GK of the new attacking team B takes up her place to throw in.
Team A leave their own opponents:

- GK and GD quickly fall back into their defending goal third
- WD and C quickly fall back to the centre third.

To mask the set up of a zone in the centre third the attacking players WA, GA and GS of team A play a man-to-man defence in team B's attacking goal third:

- GS leaves her opponent GK and takes on GD
- GA leaves her opponent GD and takes on WD
- WA leaves her opponent WD and takes on C.

The C and WD of team A in the middle of the centre third must watch closely and anticipate the moment when the ball is passed out of the goal third and into their area.

Zone defence

As soon as the ball leaves the thrower's hands, the defender nearer to the path of the ball must assess the ball's direction and trajectory, move and launch herself into the air to left or right, or forward or back to make her interception. The other player must be ready to cover her if it fails, by retiring further back, while GD and GK retire to the circle.

Example 2

Zoning the opponent's attacking goal third.

GD and GK are side by side half-way back in the goal circle to cut off the pass into the circle. WD and C are side by side as before but half-way between the transverse line and the circle to cut off the pass into the goal third. WA and GA close-mark C and WD.

A zone defence is a team strategy which can only be used by very skilful players, and which must be planned and practised and used at the most appropriate time in a match. The team must first discover the type of attack used by the opposing team. Then during the interval after the first period of play they can discuss with their Captain and Coach whether they should use a zone defence in the next quarter and if so which zone to use and in which area.

This type of zone defence can take the opposing team unawares—lead them to careless play and the loss of possession. It often takes time before the attacking team can again take the initiative and work out a way to break the zone.

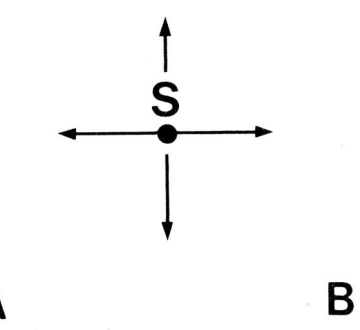

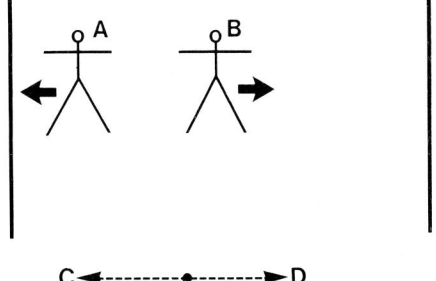

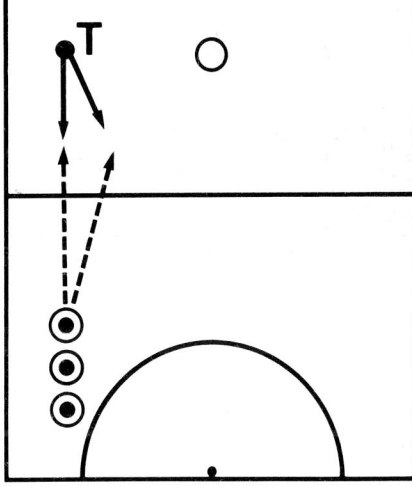

Practices

1. A and B respond as quickly as possible to direction signals given by the stationary signaller vocally or by use of hand pointing, i.e. left—right—forward—back—changing the directions in varying orders and following quickly one after the other. Both players try to keep their relationship to each other constant.

2. Two defenders stand side by side defending a goal area in front of a wall marked with lines to divide it into target areas about twenty feet (6 m) in width. The upright posts between stretches of surround netting can also be used to form the goal area.

Two attacking players, C and D, stand fifteen feet (4.5 m) or more in front of the goal, throw the ball to try and hit the fence or wall behind A and B. If C cannot find an opening, she can throw to D, who can throw back, or throw to the wall. A and B move to left and right but try to maintain the same distance between them.

3. Thrower with the ball throws a hard high pass into the goal third. The front catcher runs when the ball has left the thrower's hands and attempts to catch the pass in the centre third. Later thrower can aim the high pass to one side or the other of the line of catchers. The examples given and the practices for intercepting the pass are a simple basis for zone defence, upon which others can be worked out and developed.

The Coaching Programme

Rena Stratford with some young pupils

The teacher in a school, a club coach or the coach of an individually selected representative team at all levels must try and equip herself with as great a knowledge of the analysis of the game as possible so as to be able to dissect it into its component parts. Her aim is to help each component to be skilfully made, and to fit the components together to make a whole game, rather like the pieces of a jigsaw puzzle.

The coach must also know the Rules of the game and their interpretation, and must be a skilled Umpire. The teaching of the 'Rules' should accompany the teaching of the individual skills, gradually as the need arises.

Beginners

Teach the basic techniques of throwing, catching, shooting and getting free, which can be applied to a very simple game of two against two to advance and score with few rules and little limitation of area. Teach only one technique at a time for each skill in order to be able to observe faults.

When you develop the techniques, give players a choice and assist them in making the right choice for each situation.

Whether you are teaching an individual or a team skill, teach first **How** to do it; which is followed later by **Where**, or space, and **When**, or time, which are more difficult to learn.

A lesson should be carefully planned and prepared, and should consist of:

1. Work on general basic movement skills, e.g. running, jumping, changes in speed, direction, starts and stops—demanding quick response to directions, and providing interest, action and exhilaration.
2. The careful teaching of the skills planned for this lesson and revision of earlier work on a skill. Use balls as much as possible, and organise the class into small groups, so that every player has plenty of ball-handling practice, in the form of set drills, or in game-like situations.
3. The application of the skills practice in small team games involving ball passing, or a simplified netball game.
4. The teaching of a team skill, e.g. advancing the ball, in different areas, using the skill practised in (2) above.
5. The application of both individual and team skill in a game.

In (3) and (5) where the class is playing the game, see that all children take part. A game can be played in each of the three thirds of the court—using the width of the whole court as the length of the small courts and improvising for goal posts. When playing a game ignore all the things which go wrong, but assist the players to apply what has been presented to them during the lesson.

Try to avoid a repeated stopping of the game.

Enter the game; anticipate each move of the ball, and assist the players in making their decisions if necessary, and remind players in time so as to prevent mistakes occurring.
6. For the last five minutes, allow play to go on uninterrupted—except for umpiring—where you can. This is the time for you to assess the success of your lesson, and the progress made by each individual.

More Experienced Players

Your coaching session should contain the same elements as for beginners, i.e. general movement training, and practice of individual and team skills to improve their performance. New work should be added in game situations and applied in a full game. After the basic lessons for beginners, the next step is to absorb and develop the techniques already learnt, emphasis being given to sequences of movement, rather than separated techniques. Tactics and technique are of equal importance at this stage, but many netball players now believe they have no further use for the learning and practice of new techniques. They have a general idea of the rules, can pass and receive the ball, but are only interested in getting the ball as quickly as possible to the first player they see, ignoring correct technique, and playing without thought. This is the stage when most mistakes creep in. The coach must plan the contents of the coaching sessions so that technique training 'ties up' with tactical manoeuvres, and the students must be made to be aware that the team's scoring rate depends on successful team work, and the latter is itself dependent upon the skill of each individual player in assisting the team to keep possession of the ball.

Team Selection

Selectors called upon to select players to fill the places in a team have an extremely difficult task when a large number of candidates present themselves and the length of time allotted allows each player to be 'seen' perhaps only two or three times in games of short duration. The accurate assessment of any player for a given position in a team is made more difficult because of the 'luck element' involved. Her team play will depend a great deal on the other players playing with her. It is perhaps an easier task to select a squad of perhaps fourteen to twenty most skilful individuals. It is then the task of the coach to mould the members of the squad into teams at some stage during her training sessions. The selector, therefore, must first of all have a knowledge of the principles both of attack and defence. Secondly, the selector must discern the areas of strength and weakness of each player's

application of these principles and by these means assess one candidate's ability against others.

Principles of Attacking Skill

1. To Keep Possession
- skill in throwing
- selection of the right type of throw
 (timing, force, direction space—direct, looped, angled)
- selection of the best player to throw to
 (availability, how closely marked, in which third the action is)
- skill of receiver in moving to the right place at the right time
 (catching, anticipation, positioning, space available, timing)
- repositioning
 (to support; to be used again for the next pass or later in the attack).

2. To Score
- Skill in shooting accurately from anywhere in the circle (balance; timing, force and angle)
- skill in positioning to be certain of scoring
- tactical positioning (ability to dodge in a confined space; to jump to retrieve the ball).

Principles of Defending Skill

1. Marking—man-to-man of a player without the Ball
- with the intention of getting the ball
- with the intention of preventing the opponent receiving the ball
- with the intention of delaying the entry of a player into her operative area.

2. Marking of a Player with the Ball
- with the intention of getting the ball
- with the intention of creating problems in passing the ball.

3. Guarding an area of the court
- with the intention of intercepting the passes which enter the area (zone defence).

4. Interception to Gain or Regain Possession of the Ball
- a pass at the receiving end
- a pass at the throwing end
- a shot for goal.

Skill in defending is dependent on positioning, concentration, anticipation, quick reaction, judgement, timing.

These are the principles in which a selector must have advanced knowledge. She must also recognise potential ability—the qualities of perception and concentration. To be a brilliant performer does not necessarily enable her to recognise these qualities as a selector.

Coaching an Elite Squad

The Coach

The coach must have the right personality and qualities to inspire, interest and assist a group to realise to the full its potential.

She must be a calm and controlled person, who can handle the individuals in the group with great patience at all times, remembering that the experience is a shared one; she is not 'the boss'. She must gain the respect of her players by means of her greater knowledge of the game, her dignity, her equal interest in and understanding of every player in the group both as a personality and a player. She must be prepared both to listen to and try and sort out their personal as well as their playing problems.

The coach must demand a quick and full response to her 'demands' however hard they sound, always providing that the coach and her demands are reasonable and understood to be so.

Training

Every aspect of training is a discipline; every technique is disciplined, the game must be disciplined, and every individual taking part must learn self-discipline—in her conditioning, the use of her techniques, her mental attitudes, her organisation and her behaviour. A player who cannot discipline herself has no place in a squad of this kind. There is so much more to the training of such players than the perfecting of individual and team techniques and the application of technique to produce a skilful and well-balanced team.

The Players

The player must possess intelligence and the ability to concentrate for the duration of a match. She must acquire right attitudes: first, a willingness to co-operate with her fellow players and with her coach; secondly, a sense of sportsmanship—she must be able to 'take' any decision given against her by the umpire however wrong or biased she feels that decision to be, or any criticism by the coach. Whatever resentment she feels must never be shown, by a grimace or even a lift of the eyebrows. Umpires, players and coaches are human beings after all, and as such are liable to make mistakes, or to have a reason for any decision that may be made.

The coach must accept that she carries the responsibility to

inculcate in her players a spirit of fair play, of playing the Rules of the Game both in word and spirit.

Conditioning

To be able to undergo the long and rigorous training to reach the heights, a player must be physically fit to do so. Condition training to become generally fit, and specifically fit for netball, should consist of a programme, devised by the coach or by a professional in this field.

Such a programme aims by by specially selected exercises to improve:

Strength—by this is meant the strength of all the muscle groups of the body, but with particular attention to those muscle groups used particularly in netball:

- the leg muscles used for running at speed, for jumping and leaping
- the arm and shoulder muscles for throwing and catching the ball
- the trunk muscles, for agility movements.

Flexibility of movement for the best possible functioning of the physical and mental qualities of movement.

Dexterity—to co-ordinate movement patterns to enable the player to vary technique according to the situation.

Speed—speed of movements and speed of reaction to stimuli.

Endurance—to carry out movement over a long period of time without 'let up'. Circuit training is one of many well known and systematic methods of fitness training, which includes exercises for all the movement characteristics mentioned. A circuit of exercises can be progressed by a gradual increase in the number of times each exercise is done, or by increasing the number of circuits undertaken, or by decreasing the time taken to complete one or more circuits.

The trainer must keep a record of each player's results at each session, and her progress, for each will be working at her own level and pace. The frequency of the training sessions must also be considered.

Each player must be trained in an attempt to arrive at her peak of fitness for the match or tournament in which she is entered to take part.

The feeling for the ball, games sense, concentration and reaction time can to some extent be improved by training.

Pressure Training

Players must learn to react and overcome the pressures imposed by a strong opposition, by weather conditions, crowd behaviour, accident and frustration.

Pressure can be put upon the players during training. To cite one or two examples:

1. Hazards can be set up, such as increasing the number of defending players in an attacking situation, by the introduction of two or more players.
2. More than one ball can be used and passed in quick succession to increase the rate of recovery and a quick reaction to each succeeding pass.
3. Frequent whistling during play will increase the suddenness of change between attack and defensive play.
4. Handicaps can be imposed. All players should have constant opportunity to experience play in every playing position, so that players within a team can be interchangeable. A well-trained player should be able to play equally well in all positions.

Match Play

No team should enter the court and start play in a 'cold' state. The body must be prepared, physically and mentally for hard play from the moment the starting whistle is blown. The state of preparedness should be arrived at during a period of at least fifteen minutes before play is due to start, and is known as 'warming up'.

Jogging, running, jumping and a short series of general exercises should start the general 'warm up'. This should be followed by specific warm up to get the feel of the ball, to get one's 'eye in', by technique practice, ball passing, shooting, etc.

On completion of the 'warm up' the players should get together with the coach for a quiet period to calm nerves, to gain a mental and physical control of themselves; a condition of being able to shut out all outside disturbances and to remind each other of the team's plans when play commences. A player should never allow her opponent to distract her on the court at the line up. She is not waiting with you to carry on a conversation or pass the time of day!

Once the game has started, the coach should sit undisturbed by others, to observe both

They have reached the stars: Australia—World Champions 1971

teams' play, and to keep records of play and of shooting. It is hardly possible to make an accurate assessment by memory only. This will assist her to advise her team during the intervals, and to plan later training. She must be careful not to blame players for failures, nor allow them to blame one another. She must be prepared to listen to and answer questions, and advise the team, in an encouraging and positive way on individual or tactical play. The team should feel able to start again, both inspired and helped to improve their play. However, the coach must not shirk the task of reproving any player if she has seen or sees signs of loss of temper, or lack of control or manners in her behaviour to the opposing team, the Umpires, or indeed her own team.

At the end of a game, it is both traditional and courteous that the 'losing' team, headed by the captain, cheers and congratulates the winning team on their success, to which that team responds.
It is the duty of the Captains of both teams to thank the Umpires for their control of the match, and the duty of every player to thank her opponent for the game.

The Captain

The Captain of a team must be a player of integrity and one who has the ability to unite seven individuals into a team; for this she needs great tact and an ability to communicate with them.
Off court, she works closely with the team coach but on the court, only she can encourage, advise, remind and inspire her team to effort, for no coaching can be given by the coach from the side line.
So, finally, the results of the self-discipline trained by the coach and absorbed by the players can be seen in the control shown by them whether they be the winners or the losers, for through this experience they will all have grown in stature. Win or lose, the stars will have been reached.